We No More Sang for the Bird

We No More Sang for the Bird
A Poem of World War I

Daniel Weeks

RAGGED SKY PRESS
PRINCETON, NEW JERSEY

Copyright © 2023 Daniel J. Weeks
All rights reserved
Published by Ragged Sky Press
270 Griggs Drive, Princeton, NJ 08540
www.raggedsky.com
Library of Congress Control Number: 2023941411
ISBN: 978-1-933974-54-5
Cover and book design: Dirk Rowntree
Cover art: "The Road" by Isaac Rosenberg, courtesy of the Imperial War Museum, London.
Printed in the United States of America
First Edition

Acknowledgments

Excerpts from *We No More Sang for the Bird* were published in *The Stillwater Review*, *Middlesex: A Literary Journal*, *Illuminations*, and *This Broken Shore*.

"To the Island of Philoctetes" and "Sand in My Pocket" appeared in *Middlesex: A Literary Journal*.

"To the Island of Philoctetes," "Sand in My Pocket," "For Wilfred Owen," "Singing from a Lower Branch," and "Reflections on Reflections" appeared previously in Daniel Weeks, *For Now: New and Collected Poems, 1979–2017* (Eatontown, N.J.: Coleridge Institute Press, 2017).

I owe a debt of thanks to Mary Kate Azcuy, Gregg G. Brown, David Crews, and Estelle Bajou for comments on the long poem in progress. I am also grateful to Linda Johnston Muhlhausen and Gregg G. Brown of the Red Bank River Read for providing a venue where I could read many segments of this book before a live audience, and to Ellen Foos, Arlene Weiner, and Dirk Rowntree at Ragged Sky Press for the care they took in bringing *We No More Sang for the Bird* to press. But my chief thanks are reserved for my wife, Jackie, son, Jared, and daughter, Rachel, who, during the coronavirus lockdown in New Jersey, allowed me to read to them the entire text of *We No More Sang for the Bird* and made many helpful suggestions for revision.

*To the memory of my great-grandfather
William Waterworth (1889–1963),
who served during the war
as a petrol lorry driver with the British Army in Salonika*

Contents

We No More Sang for the Bird
Book One: Invocations and Insistencies   3
Book Two: Rupert Brooke   9
Book Three: T. E. Hulme   25
Book Four: Wilfred Owen   39
Book Five: Edward Thomas   73
Book Six: Isaac Rosenberg   89
Book Seven: Envoi   111

Hymns
To the Island of Philoctetes   119
Sand in My Pocket   123
For Wilfred Owen   130
Singing from a Lower Branch   132
Reflections on Reflections   135
Struck from the Chill of the World   142

Notes   145
Bibliography   167
About the Author   169

We No More Sang for the Bird

Book One

Invocations
and
Insistencies

1. Preamble

Myriad tongues
were then unsung
as if the gods
grew wroth at poetry
and lay mute or blind
behind heaven's veil
while a whole world reeled
and sank beneath
the olive-hued
Newtonian wave.

2. Gavrilo Princip

Wagging his finger
like a lame god
in Sarajevo's
Franz Joseph Street,
Princip, little Gavro,
a man as low as we,
pierced the imperial
side and neck and laid
the Archduke in his grave.
So, royal flesh,
like any fisherfolk's,
drinks in lead.

The duchess, too,
Gavro's regret, pitched
forward, ears numb
to her husband's
last command: "Soferl,
Soferl, don't die. Live
for my children."

Blood on the Archduke's mouth,
blood on the collar,
trails of blood on the Russian snow,
pools in the French countryside.
And the blackbirds flew
up in wild gyres to the June sky.

What might one divine
from a flight of birds? Was there
a failure of hecatombs
or vows? Kalkhas, visionary
of hell, did you foresee
calamity in the terrible
gray eyes of Athena—and
remember that her promises
to Achilles were never kept?

Oh, little Gavro, no
child of his majesty
but our new Ares, fit
to cut the crown's jugular
and set the world to war.

Like some diminutive Milos Obilic,
Serb assassin who slew the swart Sultan
in the field of blackbirds, comes
Gavro, dreamy ascetic, draining
cups of blood-dark coffee
in Belgrade cafes, waiting for
weapons, meeting with schoolboys
like himself, hoping for glory, for history
to come to him as seductively as Aphrodite
to Anchises. Gavro, you
were living out a life in legends
the wise call crazy,
but your dream
broke the world.

And yet, to some you are a hero.
I hear the singing of a saw on bone.
Peasant Princip, born
in the rich green valley
below Dinara's height
in Bosnia, long your homeland,
which hoped to haul itself like
cordwood into a newer world.

Once the Turkish boots were lifted,
it was the Austrians' turn
to step on the kmets' necks,
to keep the rebellious
zadrugas down. Meanwhile,
the Princips, crafty border ruffians,
would wait to ambush brigands in
the high western woods.

Todor, legendary headman
of the Princip tribe, would ride
his large white horse through villages
and terrorize the Catholic girls—big-boned,
brazen Todor of the wide shoulders
astride his stallion
in his colorful native clothes,
peacock feathers jouncing in his cap and
a silver breastplate riding lightly on
his form. If any objected to his thievery,
his short musket made
short reply, and then
the knife blade poured from out
the gaily colored cummerbund
to pluck out an eye,
a grisly trophy to display
among mates, a joke to tell between
big gulps of rich Dalmatian wine.

Book Two

↑
―――――――――――――――

Rupert Brooke

―――――――――――――――
↓

1. Safe in Cambridge, 1914

Brooke, with all the small anxieties
of the young, made within a busy bollox,
though without he seemed serene
as any sun god, lolling, white-collared,
on close-cropped Cambridge lawns.

His pagan soul brooked no deities.
Beautiful as the bees and sweet as their
honey, the whole—from midge to star—
had no necessary meaning but what
a human thought might lend. We
were the little gods, he mused,
his nose tucked in Webster or Donne
before turning to the soft abrasions
of an English sun.

              There was such
a thing as love, but whither
to find it. Its wisps seemed
always elusive. No
sooner might he recall
the Munich nights with Ka
than the cruel smoke of dreams
would dissipate at the mind's
febrile touch.

              He knew this much:
The love of a moment outweighed
an eternity of insensate time.

But all this was before
the war, and the war
was not yet.

              That thundering
constricted every sundial,
every clock and calendar.
"It's the biggest thing in
your seventy years," he gushed.

"If Armageddon is on, one
should be there,"
particularly the poets,
sick as all get out
for any smash-up.

How should the beautiful
offer themselves to war?
The bowman, Apollo,
was deathless—not so
the masquerader, Philoctetes,
his suppurating wound still coiled
below the sun-shaped surface
of a fair-haired Fabian. Yet,
how should the lovely
and young offer themselves:
covered in ink or blood?
"It's a rotten trade, war
correspondent, when decent
folk—factory hands, engravers,
milkmen, laborers, and roustabout
boys clean from the pub—
are offering their lives."

It must be, he vowed,
to fight—anything less
an immorality: Shoot or be shot
and "To hell with the Prooshians!"

Even as the gray German
line drew hell as close
as Cambrai, the real war
lay far to the East,
something elemental, ill-
understood by anyone of
English blood or tongue—
a bird's shadow on a marble
wall, a shroud of hanging
bats deep under the blue
landscape's calm surface.

He connived a sub-lieutenancy
in the Royal Naval Volunteer
Reserve—Churchill's boys,
magic dust to throw
in the enemy's eyes.

To war! But first, Apollo,
battle-girded, slumped in
his chair at lunch
with the First Lord
and Eddie Marsh.

"The northern ports, Dunkirk
to Havre, must be held,"
said Churchill, expending lives
over tea and crumpets.

In training camp, Brooke admired
Grecian bodies, naked men bathing
in the autumn sun, and marked
the shadowmen limned in
the yellow glow of tent lights
as the bugler from a distance
blew "Lights Out."

                    Brooke and
the Ansons broke camp
and marched through
the Kentish countryside
as the band played
music-hall tunes. Dover folk
tossed apples and cheered.
The girls kissed them
and wept for the approach
of what was ominous.
To France: an ode
with light artillery.

But amid such waving throngs, his life
seemed "a flash between darknesses."

They sailed that night
over the dark rolling Channel,
and, sleek-hulled, the ship lay off
Dunkirk at dawn, like Odysseus' craft,
chocked with offerings,
riding the tide near Khryse.

As if from Athena's very
lips, word came: "We're bound
for Antwerp by train."

He thought then of Cathleen, her
gentle fingertips and black silken
hair, for whom there were to be
other lives—film and television—
things unimagined as the train
clacked through the Belgian
landscape. He recalled the vague
goodbyes—stupidities of war—
and considered how the mind makes
scales to weigh its chances.
Did Odysseus ask such questions
as he set out from Ithaca?
"Suppose I shall not
see you again, Cathleen . . ."
He looked at the words,
then out upon the passing
fields of Flanders.

2. The Fall of Antwerp, October 1914

Antwerp buzzed, a busy hive
upon the Scheldt, where diamonds
metamorphosed to real wealth. In the Groote
Markt, the guildhalls stood with flat faces
and huddled shoulders: the city
of rubious Rubens, the voluptuary,
of Bruegel's deep golden browns
and fables, of Van Dyck's
copper flashes and subtle reds.

Through serpentine medieval streets
and broad boulevards the Ansons marched,
as cheering crowds offered pippins,
chocolates, flags, and kisses:
"Vivent les Anglais!
Vivent les Anglais!"

Past Vieux-Dieux and its spire
lay wagonloads of dead, muddy
boots hanging over the wooden
wagon sides. Marching to
a dark château, Brooke, through
still unblasted trees, saw calm pools
give off a glimmering
in failing light. Stone Venuses
and Cupids stared with silent lips
in bitter air as the brigade made beds
beneath the unkempt shrubbery.

As he lay down in darkness,
thoughts drifted to his imperial
mum, the Ranee, like Leto,
silken-braided and brocaded,
untouchable somehow. Could
love be so respectable?
There seemed no telling as
sleep leeched out a nervousness
he hardly knew was there.

At first light the Ansons
filed down into the soft
collapsing earth, relief
for the weary Belgians.

Howitzers from far off barked
and blew the forts to rubble.
There was no way to fight
this distant Hector.
There was nothing to do but leave
or die. Valor could decide
nothing as the war storm
broke over the placid Scheldt.

Twenty-five miles to Saint-Gilles—
so far did German guns
chase the allies through
a frozen hellscape.
Oil, dark brown or flaming,
flowed wine-like from
the shelled tanks at Hoboken.
It rained burning petrol. Horses
and cattle sizzled by the roadside,
and smoke from burnt thighbones
choked out the bitter air.
Dantesque lakes and rivers
of petrol torched the land
and set the sky aglow
as foot-weary Brooke rode through
a cloud of refugees
who pushed forlorn handcarts
over the rutted roads—old
men broken, women with
hardened faces, children in tears
or lying down in the open
fields, too tired to feel
the sting of sharp night-cold.

In an unlit church, he found
behind a heavy door
the huddled bodies of
the living, motionless
as gargoyles in sleep.

Then, as in a dream, troop
trains came to steam them
to Bruges. They sailed
from Dunkirk in a deep
mist back to Dover.

3. Home Again

As he slumped
in a London theater seat,
an antebellum sameness
cast him beyond
the diurnal hurly-burly.
He watched with the distant sun-eye of
a newborn god
the taxis on Oxford Street,
neat ladies taking tea,
and the hawking of creased newspapers.
Yet, it might have been a simple
weariness of mind.

Laurette's song splattered
off him like rain
hitting a slicker. O
Antwerp had fallen. Could
it be he was the sole Apollo
to throw sun or plagues
across the shadows of
a crime? Or did war
just come, the fault
of nobodies written in
a universal code
at the start of all?

Petrushka at the Drury Lane
could not unwound
a blue eye from
the shadow of a half
million refugees
shivering in a mud of fire.

"Everyone ought,"
Brooke mused, "go in."

Here was a holy thing.
At last he had achieved
a Keatsian kind of beauty,

not inborn but won.
There was something
to be opposed,
an ugly opposite
from which a drowsy
loveliness arose.

Deep in a dream, he walked out
in heavy sunshine to
the lagoon of Mataia. He'd
dreamt of Taatamata,
whom he thought a suicide
for certain loss of him. Sunlight
through languorous palms
told him now the world
was his enemy—
but the bugle woke
him to a full moon
that bulged white
through the window like
a throbbing sister.

4. To the Holy City

Holy now himself and willing
to risk all future sons
to see a bitter thing opposed till done,
Brooke transferred from the Ansons
to the Hood. With pith
and pistol, he boarded
Grantully Castle to steam
through sea shift for
the ancient holy city of
Byzantium.

    About his neck
he hung the five-point amulet
a mysterious lady left ashore.
Off Spain he scented something
Andalusian, a wine-like air,

and thought of dark-eyed
Moorish lovers and entangling guitars.

On watch he saw the silver start
of dawn over dust-dry Africa,
as the moon waxed full above the tumbled bones
of Carthage. A sapphire sea
sent up spectral shapes
of triremes and quinquiremes
the sweated backs of dead men
forced through swollen waves.
Meanwhile, half a million Turks
waited in the Troad.

               Evening had fallen when
he first laid eyes on Lemnos. The *Grantully*
groaned past the gray-hulled ships—*Elizabeth,
Nelson,* and lonely *Agamemnon*—
to anchor in Mudros Bay where
Philoctetes once lay nursing
his fetid wound, his fist tight round
the remembered greatness of
the bow of Heracles. Almond
trees were everywhere in bloom
and the sheer blueness of the sea
reflected no afterboom of war. Brooke's
field glasses brought to view
Olympus, but its misty top, thicker
than thought, revealed no gods
upon the ancient rocky thrones
to whom a poet might appeal with tufted wand.

5. Wounded by a Mosquito

They took ship to Port Saïd, where soldiers
pitched their tents on the dirty marge
close to the ships and sagging docks.
Sand drifted in a churlish wind
and salted everything
to the skin. By camel Brooke toured

the tomb of Cheops and gazed
through heated air at the Sphinx's
broken nose.

                Later, with ringing ears
and a stainless blade of pain through
the temple, he lay down under canvas
to watch dust circle up from marching
feet and drift toward the sea.
The shouts of brother officers
seemed a ventriloquism of the wind.
Struck by a shaft of sun so sharp
there was no sting, he found he could
not rise.

        Sent by cab to Cairo
to recuperate, he lay in a sweat
chewing arrowroot, a strange blister
on his lip. Beneath the gauzy netting
in his drab hotel hope swelled
that he would not be left behind
like that other archer.

        As his men
shipped out to meet the Turks,
he dreamt of quiet camels,
uncomprehending of death, burdenless,
and of the everlasting human beauty
of Menkure's tomb, which
an uncomprehending thing
had brought him to.

6. To Skyros at Last, April 1915

He sent home semiprecious
stones, like Keats' "worser lyrics,"
and wearily took ship for Lemnos
with the corps. *Grantully Castle*
cruised aimlessly in rings, seeking
a lost lighter, and the dreamy

cradle of the sea rocked him
as he took to bed.

     Brooke longed
to fish a threnody from these
purple-seeming seas or, better,
net a fluttering verse from
the hot Aegean breezes.

                  Hulking
battlecruisers and barges choked
Mudros Bay, so they made
for rock-strewn Skyros
where sweet fliskouni,
flowering sage, and thyme
perfumed the sea air
off the island.

In London, St. Paul's dean quoted
Isaiah of the singed lips: "The dead
shall live, my dead bodies shall arise.
Awake and sing, ye that dwell
in the dust," then read Brooke's lines:

These are waters blown by changing winds to laughter
And lit by the rich skies all day. And after,
       Frost, with a gesture, stays the waves that dance
And wandering loveliness. He leaves a white
       Unbroken glory, a gathered radiance,
A width, a shining peace, under the night.

Brooke now mused on nothingness: The best
may be we fall to a "pulse." Or mayhap
the memory shifts itself to a bushel
of atoms arranged some other how
to mix among the dirty grains
beneath the dingy sagging
piers of Port Saïd—as a mosquito
might be formed from the mingled
blood of Philoctetes and Jesus.

Safe in his plush London parlor,
old Henry James, half a deserter
in his heart from the war that tested
whether liberty could endure,
read and reread with trance-like voice
the sonnets for the dead that he
might reach Brooke in a telepathical
communion of sublunar grief.

But the soldier did not grieve.
He wondered was it love
or pride that led to this—
a love in willing to be shot
or not to be or to fall of a fever
from a thing so small? Did it matter
as long as love lay
at the root of it?

                Broiling
beneath a Mediterranean sun,
Brooke led his men through
drills, then rested high on a hill
in the shade of an olive grove.
Skyros tumbled before him to
the sea, angular broken marble,
pink and rose, fired with
the flames of blood-red poppies.
Fathoms down, clean water showed
the silver gleams of fish
darting through green and
azure shadows as the sun
played golden along
the soft suspiring bosom of the sea.

Peace and fatigue were enemies
to Brooke, who had loved to
swim naked as a god in Byron's pool.
Now what was cool grew fever hot
and poured out at the brow,
the latent taint emboldened

with his lassitude under this
unfamiliar sun.

                Stokers
hoisted him wrapped in blankets
to the picket boat.
Transferred nearly comatose
to the *Dougay-Trouin*,
that lay quiet in Trebuki Bay,
Brooke tried to speak,
but his golden throat
proved dry of words. *"État
desespere"* was all
the surgeon could say.

Brooke lay in a swoon
when the orders came:
"GALLIPOLI," then died
in anticipation of the rest.
The uncaring sun shone
through the open cabin
door upon the white
sheet of his bunk
as a breeze moved
the ship a bit and fish flowed
unconcerned in the sequined
depths of the muttering sea.

Beneath the cloud-occluded moon,
officers who soon would suffer
bitter death or wounding from
flung metals or languid gas
lined Brooke's stony grave
with olive sprigs and flowering sage.

Old divinities seemed to stir
as young fingers lay a poet
in his grave. The night
obsequies spooked the bronze-
belled goats, which jingled
and clattered strange rhythms
more and more distantly.

Book Three

↑
───────────────

T. E. Hulme

───────────────

1. A Promise Kept, 1914

He had promised to go in.
His nature, though authoritarian,
could not brook the German kind,
even as his father's menacing strop
beat him to oppose
the threadbare purple velvet,
mauve slippers, and slipshod
nature yack of bearded Vics,
though Hulme made a fool
of Pound, too,
gullible Idaho hick.

Some claimed he was a protofascist,
big-boned Hulme with his ham face
over the garden gate like a low-hung
moon. He thought man less
than wonderful, fixed with a spot
of rot at the core—limited—though
with strictures
his clay
might shape up to something decent.

Disciplina, severitas,
industria, and *virtus* —
Roman virtues —labored
to produce *humanitas.*
A duty
to something greater
than himself made him
go in, though he saw
with an agate eye
the evil in it.

For Hulme, drawing-
room bully, yet
gentlest of soldiers, war
wove a necessary
horror and at the bottom
of it all: Adam

come a cropper.
Man couldn't help
himself to be
other than he was.

He'd promised Brooke,
if war broke, he'd go in,
so joined the Honorable
Artillery, a common private
—Company B.

He left his newfound love,
dear Kate, who'd warned him
off the street hussies and shopgirls
with whom he loved to copulate
with such gruff gusto in the dark interstices
of public byways and buildings. "Good,
my Molly, pull up yer skirts
and hold tight to the rail. I'll
ram you straight in the dank tube
station till sweat comes with a wail
or the little soldier perishes
in yer sodden trench.
Oh, my lovely lass."

And then came Kate,
raven-haired and toothsome,
straight from Rebel Art Centre
of Wyndham Lewis.
He battered her buttocks with
a knuckleduster,
and she kissed him for it.

"Oh, Katie, Katie
kiss me and never let
the yellow whiskey
touch thy lips."

At Belhus Park he took training—
bayonet, riflery, and trench—
before going down

to cold Southampton Docks.
Many an amusing girl
waved from the windows
as long green lines
of infantry marched,
all out of step, through town
down to the embarkation point.
But fewer than a dozen came
to wave them off.

With a metallic reverberation
the ship steamed over La Manche,
half a day to Havre,
two destroyers
shadowing as escort.

In France, mud was ever
the predominant impression.
They slept wet at base camp,
twelve to a tent, till dawn
revealed the stocks of rum
and victuals readied for
the front. Trucked
to the trenches
like crated cans or cattle,
the troops endured
their first shellburst—
a locomotive high
in the sky, then
a silent puff of black.
Only after came the bang
and a kind of shrill whistling.

Hulme's company sheltered in
old barns from winter rain
and slogged across fields and farmyards
with mud-topped ankles and
heavy soles. They heard
the English batteries bark and thud
and the enemy's rejoinder.

Later they lay under the broken
panes of a vintner's greenhouse
amid the woody vines of Bacchus.
And in the evening, Hulme could hear
heavy guns going off in distances
with the sound of summer thunder.

He volunteered to carry wood
down to the trenches
and waded through liquid
the night made brown,
watching starburst shells,
those temporary suns,
light up a blasted earthscape.

In the shower of lurid
light, he felt as he were naked
in the streets of Piccadilly.

When star shells hung aloft the dark,
forging new noons, illuminated troops
laboring over the puddinged earth
cast down their faces so none
would seem a moon
before a sniper's eye.

He went into the trench
himself then, three days in,
four days out, and lived
between boredom and
barrage, far from Frith Street and
the Venetian splendor
of Mrs. Kibblewhite's salon.

In the wretched trenches near Kemmel,
a slurry of mud and stench, no
wire protected them in front, though behind,
the high starched collar of the stiff parado
prevented any glimpse of
a soldier's silhouette
against the sky, a mute savior

built upon the heaped-up bodies
of the forlorn dead.

He looked at his feet
and he looked at
the mud and he looked
at the low-slung corrugated
roof. The shellbursts
seemed like fiery palms
waving in a tropical heaven
until the bits of shrapnel
hit. An unlucky one
lost an arm, his head
popped off, and brains
were strewn roundabout
like rashers in a pan.
One night the steel rain
came cracking its vicious
whips so thick
even the battle-hardened
threw themselves in the mothering
mud, wailing and trembling, while Hulme,
impassive as the Buddha,
picked up a sizzling bullet
from the mire near his shoe.

2. His Blighty, Spring 1915

Chapel-billeted for a day of rest,
he watched the sand-pale soldiers sleeping
near the altar rails, their silent rifles
resting on the altar top
or slung about
the sacred statues of the saints.

Back in the living grave,
small somethings sang overhead like winter
bees above a bean flower
as the trench top froze.
One per minute,

the bullets bit a sandbag on
the parapet and spit dirt upon
Hulme's bread and yellow butter.

Boredom nearly broke him.
He bent but never splintered.
"As long as I don't get hurt,"
he wrote, "or
it doesn't rain too much,
I don't mind
this life at all."

The sublunar mud between
the lines was full of dead things,
rats, beeves, birds, and
the skeletons of horses,
though just beyond the raw lips
of disfigured earth, Hulme spied
rows of turnip leaves
waving their green fingers to the sun,
as if the shallow-buried dead
required now a rescuing or
meant to warn them off the war.

Rumors flew:
The tennis champ
Ken Powell was killed.
"It seems a waste," said one.
"Kenneth Powell
carrying corrugated iron up."
Hulme could only nod a bit
above his bent tin ration cup.

Wet all through,
he awaited the relief,
so late in coming, when
suddenly a shellburst
lifted the dark to reveal
the soldiers kneeling immobile
in a field, supplicant
to the holy thunder of
the field artillery.

One night he lugged
back from the front
a dead man—shot
through the heart.
Like an Ajax clad in wool,
he bore the cold
corpse shoulder-high.
*His face is very
near my own,* thought Hulme,
glad not to have known him.

Another day an untouched farm some distance off
reminded him of Gratton, curiously quiet,
when all at once an unbirdlike whistling overhead
foreshadowed a bursting above the tiled roof
and left red plumes of dusty smoke to drift up
from the burning house. Four
further shells sent pigs and poultry
cascading from the courtyard, and then a few dazed
soldiers, shadowed in sun and smoke,
came creeping along the ridge road,
like ants from a sugar box. Shells
pummeled the roofs of outbuildings
and barns, all set afire with
rouged licks of flame, a new
little Ilium, and soon Tommies
by the hundreds came inching
wearily along the hedgerow
and road, ammunition in the barn
popping off the while like unremitting rifle fire.

He missed her then,
her soft and sucking
wetness unlike
this other earthly wet.

"Oh, Katie, Katie
kiss me and never let
the yellow whiskey
wet thy lips."

War was a kind of laboring,
digging and waiting and lugging
the dead, an oscillation between
the brilliant reds of riven flesh
and a brown, mud-borne bore.
No arm needed to be steeled
for the spear, no wrist made stiff
for the bow. "There is nothing
to do," said Hulme, "but to go on."

Then, when the lilacs bloomed,
tout à coup, Hulme earned his blighty,
shot through the elbow near St. Eloi,
a flesh wound for a philosopher.

3. Convalescent

At St. Mark's Hospital, Chelsea,
he read his Kant in "Chermun"
while the elbow healed, stuck
as he was amid sick and wounded
and white-skirted comely nurses
who thought his choice of books
impolitic or just plain bad.

Once convalesced, he wandered
old haunts, lonely for his
far-flung chums. In the Café
Royal, where white-tied waiters
still slid coffee and crumpets
across the tomb-like tabletops,
no politics or poetics reverberated now.
Amid whispers in the quiet room,
where his voice had once boomed forth between
the parquet floor and coffered ceiling,
his mind impastoed translucent faces
of absent friends— Bevan, Curle, and Nevinson,
Ramiro de Maeztu—all
in their accustomed places seeming,
until their features faded from his view.

The War Office lost him in the shuffle.
He never was called back.
This gift of time Hulme used to chide
the pacifists who damned
all wars from Troy to this.
"All things were ending always,"
or so Hulme said. No war
could ever hold things up, and yet he knew
it mattered to which end things tend.
A German hegemony would never do.

This unlooked-for peace,
far from the rifle's crack
and the liquid smack of bullets
in the mud, abruptly broke
with news his good friend
Gaudier-Brzeska,
the sculptor, was dead.

So, though all reasons
for this shindy's start
seemed hollow now,
Hulme, himself unbellicose,
went back in, an old Roman
warning Russell—"Many false
reasons can be given
for true things."

4. Belgium 1917

"I've had my share
of the trenches, I think,"
Hulme penned Eddie Marsh,
feeling impotent against
the general staff's
entrenched stupidity.
He wanted a commission
in the Marine Artillery, a small
say in how the war was run.

Hulme somehow wangled
one—and with his thick
wooden box of German books
shuttled first to Portsmouth,
then farther up the coast
to highland Cromarty,
a new-minted second *left-tenant*
tasked with discipline, gunnery,
and guarding the gray-hulled fleet
that rode the tide near the rocky
shore of remote South Sutor.

In a little hilltop hut, he
scratched out essays on Epstein
as the men played upon the flinty
cricket pitch that sloped down to the sea.

He daydreamed of Katie sucking
the salty nectar and saw her floating
weightless before him as he stuck
his tongue inside her weeping flesh.

And there were times he met her furtively
in secluded stuffy rooms. The sex drowned
gloom and stanched the fear
of disappearing. Between times,
she dashed off "hot" letters to keep
his blood in percolation. Hulme
wanted sex as solid as sculpture, hard
as marble, asserting its beauty—the cult
of a god hardened and real. But war
put in its caveat, and he put off marriage,
never wanting to leave a widow.

Too soon he found himself serving siege guns
along the Belgian shore—"Eastney"
and "Carnac" batteries, and his, good old
"Barbara," closest to the German line
near Nieuport Bains. Their mission: soften
up the Germans for an assault at Passchendaele.

A sandscape surrounded him with
the sound and scent of summer holidays,
dissolving utterly the sordidness of war.
In the distance he spied white breakers washing
toward him like time itself. There
were easy chairs in the coastal cabins—
and electric lights, no less! He wrote and read
in bed, though shells burst near. And sometimes
great horns would blow to warn
of mustard gas, the men emerging then,
masked like swarming insects, choked
and vision-dimmed, to man the guns.

Under ordinary duress, Hulme abstained
from the ration of rum, never wishing
to dull his wits. And having seen
his share of scientific death, concluded,
nonetheless, a scientific remedy for war
was best, even while he proclaimed
every child a desire made manifest.

Each day shells fell near. The enemy
well knew where the British heavies lay.
So Hulme prayed for bad weather to blind
the spotter planes. He had escaped,
after all, by some secret twist of fate
to the artillery so as not to be made
fodder by the folly of other men.

When not with the gun, life seemed
strangely sedate. He billeted in
a long wooden bungalow overlooking the sea,
like a banker on holiday—far
from the trench's mud, vermin, and ordure.

                                          But too soon,
the gunners were exposed. Counter-battery fire
killed the Carnac crew, and other mates succumbed
to gas. As the odds against him grew, Hume turned
to thoughts of carnal bliss. Would Katie send
a photo of herself bereft of stitches to keep his head

on something else? He composed summer idylls—
Katie in a cotton shirt with naught above
her stocking tops. He longed to feel another
English summer in her cupped heat, to sheathe
himself again in her soft willingness.

Having borne for months drumfire and gas,
Hulme earned a pass to visit her in London—
just one night in a secret lair where
he folded into her, then dressed
and stood a long time in the doorway
to watch her as she lay love-warm in
the unfamiliar bed. "I can't swallow" is all
he said, then turned away.

                                            Back with his gun
one dull Friday in early fall, he somehow
missed the sound. The others, hearing,
hit the dirt or ran, but Hulme stayed stock still, erect.
Gazing skyward, a sudden thought
suspended him from time. In that frozen
moment, a shell caught him square
and burst, leaving little of
this one desire made manifest,
forsaken or accursed. But closed
up in his khaki pocket, a verse survived,
culled from *The Book of Common Prayer:*
"Thou only art immortal,
The Creator and maker of man."

Book Four

↑
_____

Wilfred Owen
_____
↓

1. In England

Oh, little Wilfred dutifully read the Bible with his mum
and bumped about bricked-in Birkenhead
with verses effervescing in his head.

After school, cocooned in blankets
in his attic room, he'd read
the *Fairie Queene* by candlelight
as his brother tossed sleeplessly
the whole night through. But there would be
darker days than those in Willmer Road,
where mythic harridans heckled and bawled
at the uppity Owen boys.

Though his father was but a station man
on the great railway, Wilfred fancied himself
a manor lord. His mother hoped he'd be
a country vicar, sauntering serenely through
a walled garden of grimy souls, secure in
his living, but his disposition toward
the boys and the thought that God
was naught but a piper's ditty pricked
a conscience discomfited with the false.

An apprenticeship at the vicarage had him
tinker with fallen souls. While he admonished,
he read the verse subversive hidden away behind
the hymn books. True poets, he mused, must pity.

A dutiful soldier of the gospel holy, he tented
at Keswick camp meeting, shifting
all night beneath damp blankets, the bicycle
of his escape rusting in the rain. The bleating
of much freer sheep beat in his ears while he
suffered in silence, the revival he craved
eluding him like a swift girl along
a country lane even as he baptized
himself in Derwentwater and slept
in the shadow of England's holiest bard.

He was confused in love, drawn by
Vivian, the bricklayer's boy,
yet flattered too by the flirtatious eye
of the pretty Milly Montague.
Perhaps her soft hands could purge
the fire in his mind, though he dared not
imagine even the shyest kiss. When
she turned toward him in a daydream,
she suddenly had Vivian's eyes and her
warm hands became the boy's, fingers
massaging the ribbed piano keys
at *his* surreptitious lessons.

2. In France, 1913–1914

As he boarded the steamer to France,
the bodies of children hurled
from a farm cart in Dunsden Green
through a miracle of sunlit space
seemed ever-imaged in his dreams.
He had fled not so much these angelic
dead, who had thudded back to earth
from their own brief flight,
but the tightening collar of the dreaded
church. So off he went to teach
English for a pittance in Bordeaux.

One morning Poincaré arrived in that sunny city
to consecrate a monument to the dead
of seventy, *Victi sed in Gloria* graved
like lead on the stony plinth, while above
a bronze-cold France bore in her muscled arms
a naked soldier gasping out his last.

Wilfred ambled up the ship-lined Garonne
and in polite company hinted
his father was a baron. Off days,
he sat annoyed in the Christian Union Club
as ham-fisted Germans played
dancehall tunes on the ribald upright.

The watched and warded Henriette, a stunner,
longed for his stingy lips. But Wilfred's eyes
were on her would-be lover. And though he warmed
to her once she took his arm for woodland rambles
on desultory summer afternoons, her glance froze him
as he heard the hideous wings of Eros beat
about him in the humid air. With Henriette's
heated hands upon his cheeks, he asked
if passion's flame burnt even memories—
the hymn books, confessionals, and letters of the dead?

Her shining eyes bid his heart to overbeat,
though he longed more to lay asleep
upon the strong, pale shoulder
of the *dieu mechant,* holding
that all women's beauty drew him
to clasp what beauty moves to be—
the gorgon, dissipate sugar,
and over-the-hill hookers waiting
to take their tithe close by Russell Square.
In lieu of these, Wilfred retired
to his stifling lair in the Rue Porte-Dijeaux
and hid himself under myth.

At Bagnères, where Escoula's music uprose
in stone, rousing cotton-white, sun-drunk houses,
he sat with one knee over the other, a new Théophile,
wildly insouciant in the garden of the *sylphide,*
Madame Léger. At times he strolled along
the verdant byway with parted hair and polished shoes,
listening to Tailhade pour soft sibilants into his ear.

Other days, he strode along the sun-bright hilltops
gazing at the long backbone of the Pyrenees, or bathed
away a smoldering malaise in a secret pool
of mountain runoff too cold for the heats of Eros.

Then came word of the archduke's undoing,
just a notice in the news as calm as paper and
so far away, like history already ancient. But soon
young men began reporting to their regiments

while Wilfred languished, smoking Egyptian
cigarettes in the quiet garden of Bagnères.

A world away the war unfolded in new thunders
and the clanking of machines, but he lay back
asleep in the shade of a white birch tree,
until the cranky sun, slanting West, awakened him,
newspaper ink still smudged upon his thumb.

On came the first freshet—*La Guerre Sacrée*—
like all wars, piping its orisons and organ music
from the hollows of femur bones. And in Bagnères,
women, awake to its tune, were weeping in the streets.

While the dead queued in ink-black columns, conscripts
queued themselves, farms losing laborers to
a new harvest. In the shops, costs were up, and bread
went wanting, though the mounting dead craved none.
All foreigners were fingered. Suspicious eyes
cast wonder on him—spy or shirker?

As evening flushed out the sun, Wilfred, amazed
at the unreal swirl, gazed again toward neutral Spain,
wondering if he might find his refuge there.

The ill-intoned
patriotic songs
the town band played
in the public square
brought back to him
the boyhood soldier games
in Birkenhead. He longed
now to be arrayed
against the Hun, a hero
of the eastern front
who still might sprint
home for lunch
with dear-old Mum.

In unguarded hours,
he dreamily absorbed

Tailhade's ancient rallying cry:
French youth were destined
to defend the bright culture their
living blood still stored,
expressed in the tongue of
crystal and gold. A right ideal,
thought Owen, run ripple-like
into his hyacinth ear, the meek advance
of a swelling tide to keep him
from fracturing in the face
of fear. He might still find
himself a soldier armed
with lines from the *Fairie Queene*,
defending his language in
a fetid trench. Yet he held back,
reasoning a poet alive worth more
than a dumb soldier slumped in his grave.

The deflowering in Flanders made life
dearer as he set himself above the hoi polloi
for whom war might prove a "useful weeding."

And then some timely contretemps
pushed him from Bagnères (had Madame
Léger pressed desire too far?). He fled
back to Bordeaux but found
the railway cars choked with military freight—
the broken bodies of the captured Hun.

Parisians, Poincaré, and the senate, too,
had fled to the southern city, where ladies of the metropole
smartly strolled, meeting every glance. Anxiety's
more orderly contra dance of neat flesh led Owen to think
again of Helen: *Was it beautiful women for which men bled?*

In a converted school, he observed surgeries
on wounded men,
where blood dried over
the innocent ink stains on the floor.
His clinical eye described
the gruesome wounds, readying his sense

for war—inured, he thought,
to the screams of the unanaesthesized,
their flesh carved carefully as a roast.
Perhaps it was the pain graven on
the face of youth and in those eyes
that made him amorous for boys.

On All Soul's Day the bells beat bronze
for the unalive as he pondered, snug in his *chambre*,
the pain and pleasure of desire, how a French boy's eyes or
a face—Vivian's—could make him drunk
with fatal loveliness. Self-satisfied, he
won his living teaching English to the French, until
some strange news, like a gentle tide, drew him
inexorably in: Tailhade and Anatole France had volunteered.

U-boats were sinking channel ships, and France
teetered on the brink, but still he wouldn't risk himself.
He took to tutoring rich boys—English grammar, Latin,
Shakespeare, history, and mathematics. After dinner
there were Catholic prayers, and then he sat up
smoking and chatting with the mademoiselle
before retiring to his cell to scan fresh lists of dead.

At Sunday mass he scoffed at the candle,
book, and bell but well watched the darling acolytes
who held the silver crucifix for the faithful to kiss.
He dreamed his own lips would miss the chill
silver and brush the boys' hot skin.

And later in Calais, finally homeward-headed,
he stood oddly out against the tide of Tommies
sweeping in—all accoutered
with new packs, puttees, and helmets—
brown leather straps buckled tight
beneath their chins.

3. To London and Back, 1915

He seemed a stranger in London,
a stranger to himself, though
somehow happy to be home,
where to comfort the afraid
re-laid paving stones patched damage
Zeppelin bombs had made.

Meantime, recruiting posters
pestered: "Why Aren't YOU
in Khaki?" He scarcely knew,
puttering about in business broadcloth.
He spent two nights wandering
the grimed streets of the Jewish quarter,
keeping silent company with bearded rabbis
and small-time businessmen,
a somber Sabbath-keeping.
There, the thumbprint of a Zeppelin
shadowed the pale night sky before
slinking back across the channel.
Still, Wilfred hesitated to go in,
brooding instead over the bulletin
on the hotel notice board—
the Artists Rifles wanted men.

He returned to France convinced
he should enlist, a volunteer defender
of the rolling countryside and patchwork
farms his train clacked past,
a defender of his mother-tongue,
though insistencies soon melted back
to the listlessness of life
beneath a southern sun.

An occasional intense desire to fight
left him full of inner peace, though he
thought training's tedium
only worth it if the war should last.
Then, years hence he should offer
no excuse for staying out but write

himself another story.
Dulce et decorum est
pro patria mori.

4. London Again, September 1915

London, so luminous last time,
was now blacked out. Bloomsbury
and Central London hit. Owen
drifted, a phantom of a former time
through this new-wrought Limbo,
and then produced himself fit
for a soldier at the Artists Rifles' door,
down from which stone-eyed Mars
and Minerva cast serene contempt
for flesh and fleshly things.

As Loos raged, Owen rode
the rails to Shrewsbury
for one last visit home,
then quit civilian life to kiss
the book and swear
by the Almighty God to be
a faithful soldier to the crown.

Quartered in Bloomsbury, Yeats' domicile,
he trained to be a junior officer
and after drilling, clumped up
steep narrow steps with tired legs
to hear the verse *moderne*
ring out atop Monro's
under the sign of the torch.
Here, "Poetic ladies," forgetting war,
admired his smart green uniform,
imagining him their lover as he listened
to Miss Klemantaski read Tagore.

His battalion decamped to lodge
in rustic huts in Romford
among undulant fields,

close by the country mansions
of ancient landed folk.

Here, after drill,
the commander quoted Horace,
"Dulce et decorum
est pro patria mori,"
and then Ruskin on the need
to wage "creative war,"
fit lessons for the swarthy sons
of oak-waisted Mars.

The officers imbibed this new religion,
not to serve for glory but
for duty's sake, to put
the men before themselves,
to counter fear with work,
then filed out to the frozen fields
to hurl grenades
and lead sharp marches by the stars.

An inquisitive chum, Herbert Briggs,
brought Owen to the baths
where he learned that only nakedness, not
politics, religion, nor even love,
could efface old inequalities.

There was no leave for Christmas in '15,
just lunch in his hut—custards and jellies
and dinner with new-made Romford friends.
Turkey, plum-pudding, a quick game
of charades—the plenty "overpoured."
He was happy yet found the word
"peace" jarring even said in "hushed
breath," given the scythe of war.

Later, he penned draft after draft in new rooms at Monro's
where he sipped soup and talked French
with the bookshop's maid—all while
Chopin's funeral march replayed in his head
and he saw the trenches ribbing Europe
as a titan's solemn grave.

                In the business
of war, the cadets held night marches
on Hampstead Heath, where Coleridge had pressed
the hand of Keats and felt the coldness of
impending death. But Wilfred came away
with nothing but sore feet.

                He was sent away
to officers' camp where cold snows made March
"the winter of the world," though soon enough
the almond trees, like sudden freedom,
bloomed to spite the racket of riflery
over still frigid fields.

                As darkness cast its coverlet,
cadets, the ache of the march in their calves
and feet, lay down to sleep along the creaking
floor of a commandeered old manse,
only to be knocked awake by sudden nearby booms
and blooms of light in the night sky, prefiguring
a Zeppelin, the dark-looming shadow
of a humming god heading campward
as anti-aircraft barked below. And then,
this strange menace vanished behind
a new-formed cloud
and crashed off the Kentish coast.

5. To France in Arms, January 1917

Owen's hope had been "to swoop
over the Wrekin," a newfangled Perseus
aiming to down the dragon Zep that shadowed
his sleep since Romford. But the army
clipped his wings, pinched him into
earth-bound musketry, and packed him off
to Étaples where winter gales slapped
the dunes and stunted the pines. Here,
he imagined himself stuck
in a cattleyard close to the abattoir.

                                    In his
solitary tent, he lay listening to the Scots,
drunk during Hogmanay, or to the sharp
sea wind, a voice bigger than any war, the while
discerning in men's eyes a dead
look "more terrible than terror."

When he entrained for the front, he felt
a newbie among the veteran officer corps that had
suffered on the Somme. Baptized in mud and billeted
on a stone floor, he winced at his cottage mates,
the knavish, smut-mouthed musicians of
the regimental band, whose cursing
shook the "flimsy door."

Later, bunked in his tent, he heard
for the first time the "sublime" sound
of distant guns. The resigned soldiery sang
"The Roses Round the Door" and penned
anxious letters before finally filtering
into the filthy trench. Owen found
his feelings and his feet were numb.
But he sent a coded word home
to his worried mum, S-O-M-M-E.

At Concelles, amid camouflaged guns,
he found nothing but mud and thunder
and pored over his mum's letters,
a little lifeline to normality and home,
her Edwardian hand too civil for
the warscape on the Somme.

Each night proved sleepless, a "stupendous
thunderstorm," lightning-bright. Reverberations
shook dust down in his puny hut, his boots, books,
candlesticks, and heart all jumping at each burst.

He anointed his sore feet with whale oil,
then donned his steel helmet and thigh-high
rubber waders to inspect the forward line
where German shells sent up thick showers

of red Picardy clay. Here, Owen peered
at the front through a periscope to discover
the worst chaos of this war to end all others.

At last he led his company down in the dark,
boots slopping through the sucking mud—their task:
take Serre, whatever the cost, and no retreat,
even if the Fritzies buckled the army's flanks,
dealing death with bullets, bombs, and bayonets.

Lodged deep below in an old dugout
the enemy had left, Owen and his Manchesters
huddled—desperate shades in their special Hades,
water to their knees. Should a shell blow
the entrance, this strange haven would soon,
through suffocation, become their tomb.

Bombs thudding dully above
sent tremors through the troops.
Some puked while other shat themselves,
but Owen kept his cool.

Water trickling from the door spelled
a slow deadly rise, and the sentry posted there
soon caught it when a shell bit near the opening.
Blown back, he thumped down the stairs,
crying out for Owen, who inspected
with a torn heart the boy's swollen,
squid-like eyes. Both knew then
duty done even in that dark dugout
was born of love.

6. Relief and Return

Relieved at last, he billeted with his brothers
in a broken farmstead, the snowmelt
dripping on his head and freezing air
leering like something guilty through
a shell hole in the wall.
                                        Fatigue duty

gave him a view of no-man's-land
under snow, a giant's pocked face
staring blankly at the sky, as white
as unversed paper or a soldier's blinded eyes.

But soon enough his company
crawled back into line. Silhouetted
against the landscape's white,
they saw the faces of the frozen dead,
unrecoverable beyond the trench. With nothing
to shelter them, Owen and his boys
slept on the bone-cold snow. He awoke
thinking he had come to hell only to find
one man iced out of life, more solid
than a statue.
                    Still, the whizbangs fell,
ten minutes every hour as soil rained down
from the steel sky. Ardor for life
and his mother's love
let him live. But only the thinness
of the German line cut casualties—
eight killed, twelve wounded—
a necessary sacrifice to coax
spring from its snow-fleeced cave
or perhaps, like Iphigenia,
a poignant gift to victory.

Frostbite and dysentery
sapped him, but he still had work to do,
digging new trenches in
the unforgiving snow, which he ate
by fistfuls to quench his thirst,
his impassive eye the while
on the deadest of the dead,
the smiling corpses who
at last had found their peace.

7. Haunted Winter and Spring, 1917

The Boche withdrew, and Owen
was withdrawn from his regiment
to practice riding warhorses
on the frozen fields near Crécy,
where English bowmen once
had harrowed the hapless French,
bolt by bolt, arrow by arrow.

But even so far from the front
the stench of the living and the dead
and the foul sounds of bitching soldiers
buzzed in his head—all witnessed by
the unburiable dead who sat
hushed and dreaming at his door,
urging him to eke out a new wisdom in maturer lines.

Snow vanished,
the ground thawed,
and the Manchesters marched south,
skirting Amiens, to Bouchoir,
where Owen rejoined them,
a new platoon commander,
and though he still bedded
with the men
in lice-ridden straw, his captain,
a literary man, became
his closest mate, excusing him
from fatigues if he chose
to write a sonnet.

            Entrenched
with *Punch* and E. B. Browning,
no shells or snipers found him.
His wounding came amid the search
for a missing man. In the lightless
night, he tumbled into
the remnant void of a blasted house,
cracking his head, then lying the
whole night woozy in his living tomb.
Concussion caved him—pain,

fever, sickness in the pit—
and took him finally from the front.
At the Casualty Clearing Station,
he lay confused and numb—alone.
But then his servant, Jones, brought Browning,
and soon he found himself
surrounded by his fellows,
warming hands at the camp stove
as a March snow and cold air
cut into his bones.

As his boys chased the Hun across the Somme,
Owen wandered about the sickhouse lawn
in sunny weather, his head abuzz.

Then one day, loafing along a neighboring canal,
where the surface captured snatches of white sky,
he noticed barges bringing wounded in
beneath a canopy of poplars, yet to bud,
which cast a wickerwork across the solemn water.

8. Back to the Front

He hitched rides on empty ambulances,
stopping in Amiens to buy a pistol with its clip,
and sometime later sustained a wound,
slicing a fingertip on a jagged lobster tin.
He bedded among refugees, who thought
him a young savior and god, a *nouveau*
Alexander whom they embraced and bussed.
They warned him that the Jerries
had carried off the men, burnt the farms
and villages, and choked the wells with trash.

Listening by day to strafing,
a strife too distant for bodily concern,
Owen still lay unrestful among alien bodies.
Domesticity unnerved him now. He needed
to feel again the wound steel
beneath the skin, to stand up
once more to what confronted him.

As he dressed himself in battle order—
woolen tunic and trousers, linen
shirt and woolen tie, steel helmet,
side arm and swagger stick,
his Sam Browne belt—
he sought an object for which to fight,
motherland and mother-tongue
no longer strong enough. But he
could still fight for his mum, his Hecuba,
and make himself, he thought,
a worthy Hector posted in
his own "sector of Hades."

His boots, echoing rifle shots,
took him crunching across glazed fields
to find the Manchesters, though cut up some,
victorious at Selency.
His friend Heydon, his thigh-joint
busted, was knocked out
of the war and almost out of life,
though his ball of fate
had not yet quite unwound.
Heydon, at least, was lifted
out of this slothful underworld,
which seemed to strangely lighten
with the spring, what with primrose just
peeping up in the cold forests
and a fresh landscape weirdly free
from the gravure of trenches and
the pox of shells, a lightening
that tempered by little
Owen's grief for lost soldiers.

The spent but living Tommies
dug down deep in dirt, throwing up
defenses, though no counter came.
Owen worked through the day
and through the night, fortified
on brandy and the fear
of his undoing, which whispered
ever closer now, as if the lips of

some strange goddess brushed
the helix of his ear.

In the distance, under the blank
sky, he glimpsed a cliff-like
white basilica, its roof
unburnt and stones unscarred,
rising like something holy
above St. Quentin. And below,
the powder-blue Poilus
probing slowly toward the town,
probing, probing, then turning back
in brilliant sun
before a desultory fire.

A long April brought no abatement
of raw weather, though heaven
loosed a thick coverlet of snow that
sheltered Owen and his boys
in the shadow of
a railway cut at Savy Wood—
safe until a fixed-wing spotter
spotted them one clear day
and sent in a welter of shells.

9. At Beauvois

Pulled from the line at last,
the company pushed through
a formless cloud of gas to stumble
into Beauvois, three hours before a feeble dawn
peeked through the yellow haze.
The officers shivered to sleep
on a root cellar's frozen floor,
and here Owen awoke to find a parcel
late from the loving hands at home.
He shared his solace with his mates—
sweet gingerbread his sister Mary made—
and learned his mum had measles.
Some days hence, machine-gun sputtering
broke in upon the hunkered officers' Easter tea,

and Owen clumped up the cellar stairs
in time to see a German biplane
"shuddering down" the sky.
On frostbitten feet, he tore
across stiff winter fields
to find within the winged thing
a twisted body. He filched its
blood-blotched hankerchief—his first
souvenir—a talisman conjuring news—
America was coming in,
though the Yanks
could not reach France
before the fight at Arras would commence.

10. At the Front Again, Fayet, 1917

Somehow he made it—
the slow walk over the exposed ridge
row on row, as if taunting
enemy gunners, all the brass's idea,
leaving eight killed and thirty
writhing on the ridge. Owen
looked back at them elated, having
come through unscathed,
then settled into
the all-too-shallow trench
where snipers pinged at him
as he embraced
the snowed-over ground,
stiff as a dead lover.

Nine doggèd days he lay on the line.
Nine days he bedded in wet snow;
nine days on short rations;
nine days no change of clothes
nor water for washing.
Like sullen voles beneath the dirt,
Owen's soldiers sniffed the spoiled air
of an April bereft of sun. They dug down
deeper in the sodden earth and unwound

stiff spools of wire
to make a nesting—sometimes
working in rain, sometimes
under shellfire from the heavy guns
close by the glittering basilica.

Resting one peaceless moment just
to catch his breath, safe enough, he thought,
in the railway cut
near Savy Wood, Owen
felt himself drifting off to better worlds when
out of nowhere
one whizbang burst
so near
it threw him,
as if it were the hand of Zeus,
bodily in air. He thudded back to Gaia
void of dream.

Some days and nights he languished
where the Tommies lodged him—
a dank, shallow pit roughed out of the cut,
covered in rusty corrugations.

Hour by hour Owen stared out with misted eyes,
stiller than a saint glassed up in a cathedral wall.
And the dead man opposite stared back,
his dark doll eyes neither reproachful nor bitter,
his once-buried self now pitifully exposed,
deaf to snowfall, chilled rain,
and the *cump-cump* of distant shells.
It was Gaukroger, late his friend,
who never would come consciously home again.

Lifted at last like Lazarus, Wilfred felt
well enough to march out with his men.
But each day found him dizzier
in the head, as if some immortal
had wrenched his wits away. There,
imprinted as a beloved poem, lay
the image of his late friend's face,

once living and then dead, staring
forever from its unburied burial place,
unloved, uncared for, and ultimately disgraced.

11. At Gailly

His pal Sorrell, blown up and buried alive,
was sent out, shellshocked, it was said. But Owen
stayed with the dazed undead and sat apart
when the division went out on parade.
His brother officers found him
"shaky and tremulous, confused,
peculiarly behaved." He soon
followed Sorrell out, though the colonel,
unpersuaded, counted him a coward now,
when before Wilfred never had been that afraid.

He was cast among the mental cases—
shellshocked officers and men—
the shattered, shaken hundreds at Gailly.

While spring suddenly warmed its trembling hands,
Owen traipsed the grass-rich pastures with brother officers,
feeling the sun's mother-warm fingers
on his shoulders and arms. Meantime,
orderlies placed bowls of yellow flowers
about the ward—a semblance of something lost—
as if hell would not be forever, though the guns
still spoke, indifferent to soldiers' suffering.

He worked up sonnets and themes and deemed
himself "a little mad," wracked with violent
dreams—the gassed, the squid-eyed blinded man,
the ripped and bloodied rags.

Such visions drew Owen's ire at
Christ's appropriation to the scheme of war
in sermons, tracts, and poems. The true Christ came,
he told the wizard Dr. Brown—but only
between the lines—to the maimed,

shocked, and dying during lonely hours.
The true Christ's voice never issued
from the pulpit in solemn tones
but came in conscience to calm suffering,
to console the dispossessed, never
from the powerful, but from the powerless.

12. At Craiglockhart, Edinburgh

On the western rim of the great gray city,
overlooking the Firth of Forth's
low-sweeping pewter, Craiglockhart—
a failed spa—harbored war-gloomed soldiers
within a grim and fading grandeur.
Owen's shoulders and neck prickled
that he should be mustered in among
an infernal ring of the wandering lost.
But the grounds were groomed for saunters,
the rooms clean, dinners warm, skies
free of the buzz and scream of iron,
and horizons clear of muttering guns
and rifle crack—clear of unknown things.

Though he knew a touch
of madness fine for poetry,
he sought assurance from outside
that his mind was sound,
that he was still a soldier,
still a man, though the mirror,
its silver backing partly peeled,
revealed now a different
patchwork self. Away
from the ward, civilians stared
at this newly reverent boy,
his blue armband a dead giveaway—
a sickness in the head.

In solitary hours,
he studied his shed-skin.
Was this drift of poems
nothing more than pity's
drips, the castaways
of cowardice? Did he work
them up to stitch a self,
to leech out nightmare
into the healing pool of word,
to smooth the telltale trace
of sutures over the hideous real,
unifying jagged scraps
of memory and hope?

The Scottish Dr. Brock
proposed to knit Owen back
through poems, family, landscapes,
myth—a new terra firma—
crafting a more fortunate
Antaeus who would escape
the mad Heracles of this war.
Owen, too, would be unconquerable,
so said the doc, while touch tied him to
Gaia, she who bore him from the seed
of the sea god—creating
his island English self.

In Wilfred's dreams the doctor glimpsed new myths—
the fruit of failure, brash gemstones of guilt,
which shot forth when the shell severed him
from self and Gaia, she who in her loss
contrived to bury him alive. In his bones,
Owen had always felt a sure osmosis
between nature and his mind. His task:
to find this certain balance yet another time.

His own Gaia, dear Susan, came
to see for herself the partial wreckage
of her gifted son. Her lifted veil revealed
the ash of sacrifice lying softly on her hair,
though her face, unworn by care, ignited

in him something true—one step back toward
a briarless path. And after, Owen wrote himself
back to sanity, crafting, smoothing, shaping,
paring, patching his poems—fire bells ringing changes,
reverberation of lutes, reeds, organs, and autumnal hunter's horns.

He dispensed his dark dreams in clicking ladders of pararhyme—
confronting the fear of beauty, rifling through old terrors
to find it shining there, even in the fractured panes of war—
a strange, new, calamitous beauty poured out
with lifeblood lifted from the furrows.

13. Sassoon

"He's here you know," Wilfred wrote his mum.
He meant Sassoon, the hero of the moment,
who'd cast Shakespeare in a pall, or so
young Owen thought. This same Sassoon,
sent in among the shellshocked, was labeled
neurasthenic because he'd won
the military cross then rocked the brass
with high-pitched pacifist screeds.

Owen found him in a shabby little room—
regal, or at least middle class—
a new Justinian sitting quietly on his bed,
a purple dressing gown silkily draping
his sleekness. He was polishing
not paragraphs but golf clubs,
a tall, stately, bored, self-proclaimed Uranian,
at the ready for any kind of game. The most
modern of modern men, steeled
in the most modern crucible and fated
to become Owen's ancient singing-master.
He looked serenely out of the sun,
which shone like gold on his shoulders,
and judged the lowly Owen a mere provincial
with ho-hum grammar-school speech.

The sunlight did not reveal the brittleness
forming in Sassoon's steel, fissures

nightmare and visions forced,
even if war had graved on him
a new wisdom,
wisdom he might use to cure.

And cure he did, disdainfully
sifting through Wilfred's poems, taking
words seriously even in war's wake,
noting the music they made, advising
his newfound protégé to "sweat
your guts out writing poetry."

The disciple learned to search out art
in grit and rawness, in mud and water,
in whipping wind and battle smoke,
in flesh and its disasters.

Poems were true or they were nothing,
so said a wry Sassoon, and Owen
dutifully peeled off the ethereal
like a soldier's sunburnt skin, searching out
solidity—the sober flesh, muscle, and bone—
words springing like sudden violets
from among the beetled dung.

He would fight through wire and weed
to unseal from horror a troubled beauty—
human things—poetry harvested
in fellow-feeling, in pity, and in love.

He soon learned that Sassoon shared
illicit longings he'd tamped down
in himself. The master freed them, a font
of art, music, and the steady word.
Meanwhile, Wilfred worked
on his "Anthem" under the eye
of the artifex, hoping to undoom youth
cast up from the roiling surf of war.

Having learned at last the trimming,
shaving, and tempering of craft,
Owen vowed to use his bow

to speak for every Tommy, and his
first poems now appeared in print—
though Sassoon looked squint-eyed at
these new-minted lines,
worried that they might sink his.

14. Owen's Sermon

While tittering ladies sipped whisky sours
and politicos in paneled bureaus blustered
about the glory of war, our feet grew sore
(from sunbaked dusty marches) and leather-blistered.

The Germans did not fling small stone missiles,
the kind that we as children found apt for pitching,
but such as tore through skin and bone and muscle
to rend boys' bodies beyond the surgeon's patching.

In front of the front, crouched in our muddy hole,
we listened to the whizbangs whistle and scream
and heard the fear-mad, half-hit Tommies howl,
still thinking it worse than criminal to scram.

The laws of war lay down such clever traps
to keep us sitting tight as bombshells fly
and shrapnel rips the living flesh of troops,
hardening the mind with each fresh flow

of English blood, blood that soldiers lend
forever—the grim posterity of wounds—
no interest levied on the loved homeland,
the shell of the ear deaf-singing to the winds.

15. Discharged

He seemed a "mad comet" to himself,
Sassoon's mere satellite, now
flung off into dark space
to burn true and briefly brighten
unknown and fearful worlds.

He slipped off to London
for lunch with Wilde's one-time
lover Robert Ross, bald
as a pistachio, and the mustachioed
H. G. Wells, who knew Owen's name
from "Doomed Youth" in *The Nation*.

Ross, half-antique, took Owen to
his gilded London rooms
on razor-straight Half-Moon Street,
where the board was lined with brandy, biscuits,
and Turkish cigarettes—a salon
of men who kept up artistic talk till
the wee hours bled a rich darkness
over the lush brocades and electric
lamps danced in the brandy's brown,
firing the bulbous snifters.

Next day at the Poetry Bookshop,
feeling all at once among the chosen,
Owen purchased the printed poems
of friends—Sassoon and Graves—
and chatted with slick-haired Monro,
who deigned at last to know him.

16. Back in Harness

His train labored north—
away from the front
but towards the war—
a difference between distance
and time rhythmed out
in the clack of iron tires, in the squeal
of steel-on-steel rubbed raw.
Owen detrained at Southport
where reserves readied
themselves, billeted in
the damp nostalgia of
a peacetime beach resort.

The hotel, blacked out nights,
hid itself from Zeppelin crews

on the lookout for any telltale light
as they swung beneath
the belly of their dark balloons.

Secure in his tower room,
Wilfred surveyed the forlorn beach,
where summer revelers once had
bathed, and thought he might somehow
be saved. So long a paroxysm,
he reasoned, must ultimately
exhaust itself—a sea wave on
the flinty shingle.
Or so he mused. But maybe
there would be no end,
just wave after wave
in green or gray succession
rolling over the shell-disfigured
surface of the earth.

Still, he knew, one must act
as if it would all go on and he with it.
So he browsed antiques in the little shops
and read elegies beside his smoky fire
while daytime winds rustled sand
over the windowsill. Soon
his threadbare carpets sang a grainy tune
and his teary eyes grew blind.

Owen wrote elegies of his own
but found no consolation
for himself or for the hell-bound dead.
Heaven was blank and the doomed
sheer nullities while calamitous war
offered exultation, beauty, and love—
a life-born trilogy nurtured in striving.

A small, barbed hook
beneath the skin, his commander's
charge of cowardice,
drew him back to suffer with his men,
an unsubtle tug toward redemption.
And yet, a slight fear

restrained him, so he held out hope
against doom. Perhaps
his newfound friends
stuck up in high places might ferret out
a London posting, a safe spot where he
might live to sing in pararhyme.

17. In Camp at Scarborough

A grain among grains—
he slept among the many under soiled blankets
in the long wooden huts. They were whatever
England had left—boys really
and the half-healed wounded
working stiff limbs back
to fighting trim, even as new officers
rose from the ranks to replace the gentlemen
who moldered beneath the sodden dirt in France.

As Owen readied himself with exercise
or just relaxed at tea, he fancied the Boche
a silent fog set to swallow battalions whole,
as places long held—Savy, Germaine,
and Serre—were reported to have fallen.

The new recruits were Lancashire lads
green from the mills. They spilled
themselves into bunks everywhere,
all suddenly stricken with the flu.

                But Owen himself
was fit as ever to live or die, though the flapping
tent canvas, mimicking the rattle of riflery,
spanked up unsettling visions—the hideous faces
of the dead that floated above his bed.
While his fellows died,
Owen prayed to an absent God
and wrote poems in a rented cottage room
on rural Burrage Lane. Still, his hoped-for peace
refused to bud or blossom, and the thought of blackened corpses

lumping the farm furrows near St. Quentin
haunted him even as the Yorkshire spring
coaxed the lesser celandines
to bloom along the lane.
Wordsworth's lines bloomed for him, too,
while Owen hid away in his attic room,
his own poetry springing up, achingly open
to a raw inner sun. These new blooms
dug deep in dirt, waking him
from sleep heavy-freighted.

An ever-English Antaeus, Owen now sought out his Achilles-life,
    preparing his book for it, his words
        a nesting place
           for whatever the unseen soul might be
as he prepared his dust for something other—
        that old blank heaven of empty hymns
            an "unimagined thing"
                that never quite grew real.

18. With the Manchesters at Joncourt, October 1918

It was now the Tommies' turn
to pierce the German line—
a long stretch of wired trench
rife with pillboxes and riflepits,
whole arcs of ground
machine-gun swept, and then behind,
a brace of heavy guns.

But first the British guns lay down
a deadly curtain sweeping slowly forth.
Then tanks lumbered over to the crush the wire,
though German cannon knocked out three of four
before Wilfred whistled and they all went over the top
with heavy legs, nerves sparking in their chests.

German fire and barbed wire caught his company
out between the lines. The boys scrambled for any cover
as Jones, the loyal gardener boy by Wilfred's side,
took a bullet to the skull.
He slumped down in a shell hole,
his head on Wilfred's shoulder—his hot blood
a lovely crimson drying slowly to rude iron.

As the guns at last grew quiet,
a new squadron of armor rumbled past,
and Wilfred and his men rose from their coverts
to shadow the clanking hulks.

Like a gambler pitching dice against a wall,
he cast his men against the trench,
and they soon took guns and prisoners
and hurried farther forth. And when one Jerry
lunged, Owen knocked him dead with a pistol shot.

The enemy revetment on the ridge collapsed,
but the Boche soon threw a brazen counter
against the company's left, capturing
the brick mill and abandoned farm.

A demon mad with vengeance, Owen
dashed up a rise to seize a Maxim gun,
turning it sharply on the Huns, whose bullets
buzzed at him and thudded in the clay.

The Manchesters, under cover of his machine-
gun spray, routed the enemy out. The old mill farm
was saved, though a new attack threatened
to make a grave of it as the Germans poured in
an ever-hotter fire. Owen's boys were pinched
on the ridge in a shallow trench,
miserable in wet weather, the wounded
moaning out between the lines.

Owen crept out himself and
by sudden indirection baffled
the sharpshooters, but found he

could offer no help or solace
to the living or the dead.

                          That night
all ranks, high and low, lay soaked
to the skin, wet khaki weighing on them
heavy as regret. They bedded in mud
under shellfire and the slow unfurling of
a deadly yellow fog as darkness fell.

The spent men hunkered down to endure
a long, sleepless night before relief
flashed its worried face in the murky
pre-dawn dark. Then Owen led
his ragtag remnant out
under strange stars that winked
through "air mysterious with faint gas."

19. To Oise-Sambre Canal, November 1918

They rested twelve days at Hancourt where
parades, drills, baths, and polishings,
funerals and football occupied the men
while Owen in off hours penned letters
to the parents of the lost,
the blood of Jones
still inked upon his clothes.

Otherwise, he kept to his tent,
leafing through Swinburne,
that echo of the gone. Wilfred now peered past
present calamities, seeing his future self,
a poet with a spartan London loft
and a country cottage stuffed
with books—a literary lair.

All at once with peace in the offing
and Owen's cross securely won,
the tired Manchesters were ordered back
to stem a final tide. Resolute

in the face of madness, they marched
through soupy mud past faceless villages. Here,
bloating horses sickened the steady wind,
which played unconsciously among the rubble.
Meantime, eastward, heavy guns
shivered the dim horizon.

Settling down in a cellar tucked among
the trunks of broken trees, Owen learned
the company must cross a small canal beneath
a sharp persistent fire, even as the little cloud
of armistice drifted closer by degrees.

In billet he dreamed of climbing
with his mum the shaded paths
of Haughmond Hill and awoke
to the prospect of one more
over-punctilious attack
in a wound-down, wounded war.

The dirty Oise-Sambre
beckoned like the Styx.
But when no Charon drifted up
to ferry him, Owen stood
transfixed, wondering why,
with peace looming,
he should ever give himself
to water when from birth
his element was earth?

The engineers were coolly scythed,
so Owen took up the task himself.
Out on a raft with no guide,
he sweated to lay duckboards
to someone else's hell.

A machine gun sputtered, a rifle cracked,
and the mad comet at last fell, fixed,
a bit of England speaking quietly
through blackened lips.

Book Five

↑
———————————

Edward Thomas

———————————
↓

1. Civilian, 1914–1917

In the end, a bicycle,
da Vinci's vision,
leaned riderless
against the garden gate.

But now, as he lay warm
beneath a snow-thickened roof,
Thomas knew that others lay wet
and shaken to the bone
awaiting dawn's barrage.

The declaration done, he had ridden back
to Ryton, to Frost, to picnics under
ash trees, to literary talk—with no
thought he'd be a soldier. To save
him from a tribulation, Frost
begged him to come away, but Thomas,
tempted, could not abandon England.

The war, remote, reverberated in rumor as
he watched wasps suck the sweet
from a defeated yellow apple
in the meadowlands of Gloucestershire.

Thirty-seven, three children, and long married now,
he knew he would not be called. This war was
a young man's war, a soldier's war, and yet
each moonrise, silhouetting his angular self,
brought the suffering soldier back to mind.

Artemis's swooping swifts, both arrow and bow,
the orioles, bees, and lonely aspen
trees could not soothe a bitter restlessness.
"Was there something," he asked, "to be
contented with?" as Helen grew more distant
than a spoiled picture. Daydreamy
Eleanor Farjeon, their erstwhile guest,
lent intellectual companionship
and a shy half-smile cast to the floor,

while the woman—his wife—whom he'd
seduced beneath a screen of trees,
grew lonely with the fruit of it.

No orchestra, just a rimshot
had announced this war, and
as it warmed, he turned from prose
to poetry—as if some greater
concentration were now required
to outroar motor transports, steel
steamships, rail-borne guns,
and the treble buzz of planes.

He scorned a Golden Age but took
an obdurate eye to nature, finding
it a "luxury just to be" at least a little while
among the crowfoot flowers and bees,
to hear the harsh song of the sedge-warbler,
to feel the subtle burn of an English sun
along his stiff, white collar-top.

Back home with Helen, he slumped in his study
to read rafts of limpid wartime verse. He
marshaled his own words, but they tumbled
over—loose chimney bricks in
a dinning wind. Still, he hoped
to be divinely touched, the one
to sing in "frank, clear notes" over
the low chinking of
those less than tragical. He mused
on Coleridge's lines: "There lives
nor form nor feeling in my soul
unborrowed from my country,"
and learned from the light orange
crescent moon a feeling overmastering
all other calculus: that England
never could be his unless
he lay his life at risk.

2. Enlistment

With news of Brooke at Antwerp heavy
on his ear, Thomas cycled over Gloucestershire.
Would it be the army or escape
with Frost across the sea? An invisible
Athena, he hoped, might intervene
and coo him to a proper course.

Cycling back to Coventry, he joined
the Artists Rifles, as all roads led
to France—for both the living
and the lightly dancing dead. He
telegraphed to Helen, then met her
at Steep Station in field green,
his hair cropped close, and when
they kissed she smelled the sour
khaki, so far from the sweet
scents of a poet's pipe and tweed.

They walked out wordless in
the summer sun to give
themselves again to country sounds
and wished this one walk
might be forever.

He wondered: Was it his nature to be blue?
For he knew that to love the land, one must
stand apart and hear thoughts passing over
the loved hills and combes like a cloud.

Perhaps the war would bring a true ablution
to wash industrial soot away
so peewits might sing
to a smokeless, unembittered sky.

But first it was off to camp
where officers' shouts clanging brass-like
above the crunch of drill, dusty route
marches, and hours at guard
left no time for a line or two of poetry.

He practiced map-reading
on Hampstead Heath where
Coleridge felt death in the hand
of Keats and nightingales kept
both poets wide-eyed
deep into the brightest night.

Here, Thomas dreamed
the land immortal,
though it must perforce
be blind to itself were it not
for the tenuous alive
who imaged all up
from beyond
the moon-stilled palisade.

He still could not uncode the thrush's song,
so strangely meaningful.
And with such notes ringing in
his inner ear, he volunteered
to go to France, though
he could have stayed in England,
a mundane map instructor. As reward,
his landlady evicted him
from his book-cozy country study.
So he sorted through his volumes
and burned his *billets-doux*.

Meanwhile, the pacifists
at the local school
looked down long noses at
the apostasy of Helen,
as if they really knew.

Already a ghost, he was willing
to prove his love, striding along
the long green road toward
an opaque, eternal nothing.

He schooled himself in heavy guns,
accoutrements, coordinates, and logarithms,

while poems came in a steady
secret rain, well-hid from other soldiers.

He visited his family in the drafty house
set amid hornbeams, hollies, bracken, and heather
atop a hill in High Beech. Helen cooked
on a primus—there was no stove—and dinner done,
sat staring at the fire, a chill about her heart
that no flame warmed. She listened to the *chink-
chink* of Edward's axe as he cut a cord
of wood to keep her and the children snug
the winter through.

            Assigned to
a battery set to embark,
a last-minute reprieve
sent him home for Christmas.
Helen and the kids
danced in a ring,
singing at the news.

The snow feathered deep,
then crystalline
about the house.
Helen and the children
brought holly, ivy,
and evergreen inside
to make all festive
and dug out
a tiny tree to
decorate
with little toys
and candles.

Last leave he sang
Welsh songs and bathed
Myfanwy, the littlest,
before the fire. That last
night after Helen retired,
he kissed shy Eleanor
and next dawn

with Helen took
a last walk through
a bluish mist
that brushed the brittle snow.

At last, some parting gifts she gave—
a sleeping bag, gauntlet
gloves, the sonnets
of the bard.

3. Shoving Off

The siege batteries and crews gathered
on the frozen downs, readied for France.
As resolute as Hector, Thomas awaited fate
with winter drizzle freezing the grasses white
and all the farm roads shellacked in opaque ice.
The night a-glitter, he watched two vagrants
roast an animal on a slow spit and wandered
by thatched barns and ivied ash trees that, leafless,
seemed hung with living string. A rusting
thresher wheezed quiet as the frost, and
ancient milestones were lichened over
with beaten gold and verdigris.

New boots chafed deadened ankles
as he trudged about the frosty downs,
lonely under a newborn moon and stingy stars.
He watched a fox play among
snowy hills and bicycled
over hedgeless roads edged
with silent juniper and thorn. Back
in the toasty hut, he rocked
with loud laughter at the imbecile jests
of brother officers—Horton and Smith.
Then, in the chill dark, the men marched
down to the way station singing "Pack
Up Your Troubles" till a frigid car
carried them off with neither tea nor
anything to eat. A tear came then—
to be leaving England.

                    At Southampton
docks ice bobbed gray-white
in black water, and gulls flew
crying to the dark forest beyond.
The men played Scottish rugger
or danced to concertinas in
a big shed between the railway
and water. At seven they sailed
in the failing light, the dark-hulled
Mona's Queen chugging out
channel-ward, the gulls, out from
the far forest, alighting on the chill
water to watch them go, bobbing, too,
like ice near the bow and fantail.

Well-berthed, Thomas lay quiet,
one ear tuned to the men beyond
the door, who laughed and talked
of fucking, lovely fucking, as the ship
shivered over La Manche to Havre.

4. At Havre, January 1917

They slept twelve to a tent with just
two blankets each, all water frozen in the taps.
Thomas watched a luckier light
cast down from the windows of tall
houses and from stars above
the snowscape.

              He read Shakespeare
in the evenings. And having seen a young
captain kissing a French waitress over tea,
thought to warn the Tommies of VD.

                    The wounded,
streaming in by train, brought news of the move
to Neuve-Chapelle. The army had pushed back the Huns,
and he hoped to play his part, but the guns had yet to come.

The great quays of Havre now held the commerce
of war: hay heaped up for horses, cotton, and cattle
on the hoof. Hooded Poilus stood guard, their long
curved bayonets catching fire from the winter moon.
And Thomas bided time, eating cheese and marmalade,
content in his freezing tent to reread the sonnets of the bard.

5. A Lark at Last

Buckling on the bronze of war, Thomas
and the troops joked and sang as
the train waited the signal to depart, and when
the cars first lurched, the rhythming wheels
were overborne by a hearty "hurrah." Then
silence drew over them as they saw the long
platform of trampled snow and electric lights
drift back and disappear. Snow fell
the morning through along the wooded
chalk hills and covered over farm villages,
poplar trees, and orchards. At
Mondicourt detrained soldiers crunched
over frozen farmyards to billet in
half-ruined barns.

                En route again to Arras, Thomas
spotted a German biplane, moth-like among
the lovely shrapnel bursts. He rode through
a snow-muffled countryside and later rigged up
a table in the empty echo of a house to eat
off borrowed crockery. Night loomed and languished
as the heavy guns boomed, warding off
sleep's balm.

                Another night in bitter air they billeted
along the shell-pocked Arras road and dined
on white wine and cheese with mortar battery officers.
Later, digging latrines, Thomas found a dead Tommy
tucked under a railway span. The snowed-over
landscape seemed a dead thing, too. Among
broken posts, sprung droopy wires, and blasted

trees, the dug-in soldiers vanished in the snowscape
to await a thaw.

        More moles than men, Thomas
and his troops burrowed into an orchard near Arras
as a gramophone scratchily sang "Wait Till I'm
As Old As Father." Then came the thunder
and flash of the cannonade off to the south.

As fate hovered thickly over them like the blue
shadows of winter branches, Thomas
besought some living thing, some thaw
under the stinging winter wind and war, but found
only a corpse in sackcloth, snowed over,
an ancient saint dusty with heaven.
Then at dawn's light, a quivering hare,
a partridge, and wild ducks—Eostre's brood—
searching sustenance in a torn field,
enlivened raw eyes drawn up from
a military map. Ears, too, opened to
the smaller sounds of life beneath the guns' roar
and peppery ruffs of small-arms fire that threshed
both men and wheat. Black-headed buntings' squawks
and rooks' caws soon made the white puffs
of shrapnel near the high-flown German planes
more lovely still, and as he slunk along
the frozen trench bottom, he relished
the scratch and rustle of dead campion umbels
and winter whitened grass, skeletal upon
his helmet's steel.

        One starlit night when only
rifle fire broke through a stillness, Thomas's
aide, who lit the fire, said, "We're all alike, sir,
all human," and the cold wore off all thought
of class, all alike enlisting for a bitterness.

One morning he strained his neck to watch
the warplanes hover and wheel in a hazy sky
as kestrels might over Ludcombe. The lazy
circling reeled his mind back to Eleanor,

to Helen, and to home. And all the while,
stout, earthbound women hung shirts
and sheets out to dry on the barbed
entanglements strung across the road.

Arras itself was empty,
the small, white, well-ordered
square ruined in a rain
of shells. In one high house
the upper story lay exposed,
a plush fauteuil,
garment draped
as it was before the shell struck,
awaiting its absent owner.

That late February, no thrushes sang,
though a chaffinch chinked
in the chestnut behind the lines,
and nightly machine guns sounded
like a stranger's frantic
knock upon the door.

                    No larks, but
partridges next day were "twanging" in the fields,
a countermelody to the trench-bound troops
who sang "It's nice to get up in the morning"
as they marched through. Thomas toured
the broken rues and estaminets. Wet litter,
cracked window glass and bottles, a chipped
old crucifix, and empty chairs, all poured
out from lost houses in the Rue Jeanne d'Arc.

He wondered whether a mole ever died
shell-struck and watched two British planes
tumble out of the cold February sky, one
in flames, and later learned both aviators
were burnt to death upon alighting.

The last day of February left without any song
but the hedge-sparrow's. But March brought a bullet
shrieking near as he loafed upon a hilltop

and watched the German lines snake
through ghastly trees at Beaurains.
Birthday parcels came, which made him
muse on where he would be hit.
Then he heard the larks at last as he watched
humming planes fight and fall on fire,
one a Hun. Meanwhile, the raw March wind
made black sycamore leaves dance
a death round on an old deserted terrace.

6. Reburied

Thomas was back in the trench and under bombardment
until a lull lured rooks back to the tall trees, all black
against a creamy sky—a portent, indecipherable.

Shells hit a bit too near as he climbed
a high chimney in Arras to observe.
All around lay the Gallo-Roman town,
famed for tapestry. Here, Robespierre
was born and lived his early life
in penury, for which others later
so sharply paid. His house survived,
but German shelling shattered
the old town hall, its gothic
arched windows and soaring bell tower
no longer pointing toward
an empty heaven.

            No letters came,
so next day Thomas watched
a man, ghostlike, plough his field in a mist
in full view of the Huns, as if in a dream
there were no war. The first thrush of spring
sang then, and later bombardment troubled sleep,
though he dreamt he couldn't stay
to tea and woke to pale artillery smoke
staining the clear night sky.

At daybreak, still green water
in the moat of the citadel
mirrored white skeletons
of long dead trees.
But in this waking world,
blood-stained water filled
the shell craters of no-man's-land,
where beer bottles lay dispirited beneath
barbed wire.

                White cordite flashed
along dark roads as Thomas rode
back to his billet. Children,
holding hands, stared hapless
at the motoring men, and dark-skinned
women stood mum near ruined barns.

Later at Achicourt, thunderous blasts
shook the house in which he lay by night,
and biplanes hummed above by day, leaving
wheel-like tracks in the white, beclouded sky.
Meanwhile, in mimickry,
the unshattered stained-glass
of the unroofed basilica cast
its loving light through
a shell hole in the nave's stone wall.

When April arrived, frosty and clear,
Thomas delighted in the muscle-ache
come from filling sandbags under
a nearer sun and loved now the chill feel
of snow-slush about his boots.
Some days later, the same spring sun,
with warmer hands, drew forth
"fine green feathers of yarrow"
to fledge the muddy
trench top.

                Easter day dawned
bright and warm, all the world awakening
while the Boche shelled Achicourt all afternoon.

One missile burst near enough for shrapnel
to scratch the nape of the poet's neck,
like an unseen twig along a forest track.

7. When Helen Heard, April 1917

The telegraph boy leaned
his red bicycle against
the rough rail near
the nurseryman's low cottage.

The sun shone over
the little village
outside Epping Forest.
"My mother knew,"

Myfanwy said,
"what that telegram
would say." The man
she'd loved among

the woodland trees
while bees sang
in the tanglewood
was dead. There

were no words,
nor tears, but
a frozen remorse
at what had seemed inevitable.

8. The Return

His things returned,
debris from something sunk—
camel hair sleeping bag,
clay pipe and shaving
kit, a pocket watch stopped
when the dud shell hit,

sonnets of Shakespeare and
the *Book of Common Prayer.*
A diary finished off
with odd words: "We no more
sang for the bird."

Book Six

↑

Isaac Rosenberg

↓

1. Penury and Paint

He was the favored one, or so he began,
sprightly of mind, though the runt
of the litter and given to grieving
his whole life through for a lost twin.

Though Bristol-born, his first tongue
was Yiddish, which clacked through
the impoverished household,
even among boarders. Though he never
learned to write it, it shivered in his ears.
English came with schooling, there in the great
commercial city of the West Country,
where Coleridge had once inveighed against
the trade in slaves and after
wounded himself with an unlikely bride.

A little later in London
Isaac crowded with his clan
against the dirty docks,
until his mother made a shrewd move.
But he remained both native and stranger,
even among his own
in better accommodations
on Jubilee Street—
a plucky loner
with a weak chin
and a barrel rimmed
with raw *oideas*, some culled
from Swinburne's gorgeousness,
more from Keats.

His boss found him too gifted
for a workaday gig, as if poets
had no need of wine or bread.
For plaint or complaint or prayer,
poor put-upon Isaac pulled paper scraps
from his pockets and declaimed poetry
to like-minded boys in the jeweler's
loupe of light beneath an East End streetlamp.

He was young still, this aspirant,
but not immune to love's ideals and idols.
Was this the Victorian in him?
When a pretty sweatshop lass
appeared at his place in the
quiet library beneath the stacks,
he competed with Bomberg
to see who might etch her best,
then yielded to his bolder friend's lust
and played the Bergerac,
sending poems to her in Bomberg's name,
though Sonia soon divined the subterfuge,
preferring still shy Isaac.

2. At the Slade, 1911

A benefactress sent him to the Slade
to while away long days
in the tobacco-splotched studio
under the humbling eye of
the drawing master Henry Tonks—
anatomy from life, portraiture,
and composition, with short respites
for lunch and tea, and then
a long walk home to Whitechapel
in company with Bomberg and Gertler,
sharing high ideas and tough talk.

Infusions of girls in overalls
and painting frocks, who slapped color
on canvases or practiced impasto,
unnerved him, making his desire shyer.
Here, in Isaac's sanctum,
Lady Diana Manners, Dora
Carrington, and Phyllis Gardiner
imposed themselves,
the last with reddish hair ablaze.

        There were
tussles, some bullying of the Jews,
but Bomberg defended them all

from slurs, his ready fists, trained
in the ring, so willing
to black an eye
or split an insolent lip.

Meantime, Isaac wondered at dabblers
from higher social classes, who wasted
precious spaces, slumming for a time
in the heart's boneshop only to return
to comfort, while he knew
he had nothing to go back to.

Ferment winged in from Paris and Berlin—
Matisse, Derain, Picasso, Braque. But
while Bomberg plunged into the new—
Cubism, Fauvism, Futurism—Isaac held back,
tethered to the seen, and clung
to the pre-Raphaelite or Impressionistic dream.
He feared his art would fritter
into mere "symbols of symbols," though Blake
soon led him to new visions.

An old chum conducted him to
the epicenter of the new—Monro's
bookshop, the haunt of Owen, too,
where Isaac declaimed his poetry, even as
the slick-haired guru talked him down.

But while his painting
looked back unruffled,
his poems seemed
the plaints of a sparrow
seeking its mate
or other unseen things.

Art was no hobbyhorse,
he soon concluded.
It demanded always
"blood and tears" and for
the testy temperament,
these dues purchased but
a narrow independence.

                    On a whim
he sent his poems to Binyon,
who was stunned to find
his post box stuffed
with lines that "haunted memory."

Lively-eyed, he heard Binyon's
modern admonition:
"be more concrete,"
as if words had mass
and weight. But Isaac's books,
published in penury,
were thin bricks
tumbling out of Narodiczky's
radical press,
just fifty at a clip.

                    And yet,
these young shoots sought
liminal spaces tucked
between dark and light—
where in the crepuscule
one might feel along the skin
the eternal rhythm's quiet throb—
a whisper in wave and wind,
in flesh and other elemental things.

3. With Eddie Marsh, 1913

The pedestaled Sonia,
with whom he'd gazed
upon the sacred iconography
of the mage, forsook him
for a friend's bed,
her betrayal manifest in
a swelling pregnancy.
But his melancholy over lost love
was less when a friend led him,
nosewise, to Eddie Marsh
at the Café Royal—late

mise en scène of Dowson,
Beerbohm, Shaw, and Wilde,
Hulme and Lewis and free-thinking
Roger Fry.

                    Rosenberg eschewed
the decadence of imagism
and the Domino-Room rebels
who lollygagged amid frenchified
gilt and velvets. He preferred
the sublime to rough-hewn
images on which one might
bust a knuckle.
                Marsh made
him tame his strange euphony
culled from Cockney Yiddish,
and Isaac basked in Binyon's praise,
but these new literary links
couldn't pull him straight
from the muck, as short cash
finally drove him from the Slade.

4. To Cape Town, 1914

For the sake of his lungs, he said.
That's why he went. His sister
who married a Cape Town man
sent for him, for the sake of his lungs.

He took ship in steerage on borrowed cash
to cast his fate where two great
oceans clash—Cape Town—set off
by three imposing peaks
where, alien and free from
Africa's particular oppressions
and London's selfishness,
the poems and paintings
flowed out of him, more intense
than southern sunlight
along the fynbos' leaves.

He parked himself near the docks in the Jewish slums
or traipsed about town, pockets stuffed with poems,
his head with hopes, and painted
the indigenes of Cape Town with
a freer brush.
                    The rebellious
Marda Vanne, young Margueretha,
anticipating the flappers with bobbed hair
and sleek velvets, caught his breath,
and he caught her ear. She had
always loved, like him,
the wild effusions of
dowdy Camden's bearded bard
and, though never a "simple
separate person," roared
a song of herself from
the Cape Town stage.

Isaac admired her fire and took
her as his mazy muse. Was there
a little triste at the hotel
in Muizenberg of an afternoon? Did
her "heaven-dreamt" flesh
permit his "crushed life" to ebb
whitely out—
a grimy catharsis?
Who knew?

He etched her portrait—defiant and proud—
and she cast a cat's eye over his poems,
then cast him out.

                    But he turned up ha'pennywise,
a houseguest of the late prime minister's
upstart daughter, and napped in plush
appointments, awaking refreshed
to undreamt splendors—
coffee in bed, artful breakfasts,
fulsome lunches, cozy lapsangs, lavish dinners,
while irreverent flowers peeped
brightly through the window glass.

But such beauty proved a cage, the bird trill
itself a prisoner's song, and he longed
for London.

               When at last
the war news cut south to the Cape,
he deplored the senseless murdering,
though he wished the naughty Kaiser's
rumpus rudely smacked knickers-down.

As the cataclysm drew in its force
for later reckoning, Isaac sought escape.
He wondered what a war sparked in the Balkans
had to do with him. While others prayed
or enlisted, he thought God too weak or fickle
or just too blind to stop the wreck.

Instead, he filled his head with reveries
       of Margueretha who
          had given her body
and then denied it, prefiguring a deadlier seduction—
       a goddess fussy and cruel.
       She held his own desire out for bait,
until he knelt obeisant
       at bliss's altar.
And so, dream-shackled until drained
       in her "rose-deaf prison,"
he wed himself to a new godhead—one
       who saves and then condemns—
the dread, belovèd Margueretha.

5. Bound for Home, 1915

Love-spurned and talked about—
       some whispered
a "meshuggah"—he fell
       again outside
an unseen pale.

He decided to go home.

        Uncomfortable among
the Cape Town toffs,
        a burden to the poor,
Rosenberg began to miss
        the London life he once deplored.

He decided to go home.

Small as he was,
        he longed to reach
beyond himself,
        to touch a greater whole,
a limitlessness
        that spoke only
in subtle tones.

He decided to go home.

And with the whole world
        tipping its bones into the grate,
he felt himself a lonely spark
        lifted off
the furnace core—
        forever an exile
in an ever-alien world at war.

He decided to go home.

6. In London Again

More than a million allied soldiers
had perished at Mons, the Marne,
and Ypres when Isaac glimpsed
the long white sweep of searchlights
in the night sky near Dover.

He felt some pressure to go in,
though his family were firm "Tolstoyians,"
who loathed war and the Russian yoke.

His artist friends, pacifists
or objectors who

preferred prison to enlistment,
denounced the warmongers
and profiteers, lisping dissensions
while foamed-over beers
flatted before them
in coal-warmed East End pubs.

And Isaac, too, keenly recollected
the Boer War vets forlornly
begging in the streets
and rummaging refuse bins for food.
This was how old soldiers were abused
once the war was won. He held
himself an anarchist and foreknew
the whole damned thing
would end "a bloody mess."

As fighting mounted to its crest,
most homefolk dismissed all
unrelated art as little
liquid beads cast up against
a somber tide of steady death.

                        Like Owen,
Isaac thought a poet ought not
sacrifice himself in "stupid business"
but could find no way to win
a London living. No one dared risk
a few quid for poems or paintings,
though he soldiered on,
scribbling lines and daubing portraits
of those too poor to pay a fee—his father,
desperate Sonia Cohen, and himself—
the last, a lonely stab at immortality
beneath a shadowed hat brim.

7. Drawn into the Maelstrom

As crooked lists of killed
filled the papers—fresh epics

in thin black type—
Rosenberg queried: *Had God
devised a perfect evil
for me, for us, for everyone?*

Unable to make ends meet
with paint or poetry,
he felt unfit for anything,
though the "enormity" of war began
to loom larger than his mirror.

But when Zeppelins rained incendiaries
over the East End and a factory
Isaac knew collapsed in flames,
a forgotten seed in him
began to burst its shell:

If Britain were to lose, he asked,
what might I lose, too?

Still, this new Absalom,
swinging in the dirty wind,
fidgeted, fearing
the unfreedom of
"a criminal profession."

He then began to carve his own Moses—
an exemplar for himself,
an exile in his birthland—not
in marble but in
a kind of subtle wood.

He knew what the toffs did not—
that poverty sapped free will
and circumstances would prove
a trap till all he had was speech,
a small needle's gleam
beneath a tenebrous door.

All other avenues blocked,
he stifled pride as penury
bade him beg his old job back—engraver

swooning above the acid
bath that etched his lungs
as surely as it cut copper.
But this door too was locked.

Only the army, seductress or savior,
would take on any man, even slight ones
not much made for soldiering. So,
with Pound's say so
and other options out, he
embraced death to survive.

All five-foot-three of him
enlisted, one of the khakied Suffolks,
a rabble of rough scarecrows
unfit to face the Hun.

8. Training at Bury St. Edmund

Rations proved short, a hideous slop
sure to demoralize. Stiff boots
stung and blistered. But he had Donne
beside him and begged
for other books—small enough
to fit his tunic pockets.

His comrades found him diffident
and shy, aloof, and some objected
to a Jew. But he, who never
joined the army for patriotic reasons,
adjusted through regimen, routine, and work—
washing, shaving, making the bunk,
breakfast, calisthenics, drill, and k.p.,
mortars, grenades, parry and thrust,
firing Lewis guns, bayonet drill,
dinner, drill, and carrying coal,
musketry, night ops, drill and fatigues,
route marches in darkness and then back to bed
to dream of drill and drill yet again,
though a sounder sleep he'd never had
as his body grew robust.

An unsettled mind sent him back
to poetry, where interruption
played well—an expression of the real
as Rosenberg agonized out
each word, each line, scratching
out on little scraps his *Moses*,
the human hero, a ladies' man
and leader. Yearning for free
air to breathe, he knew
what it meant to be a kind of slave,
bent under the lash of discipline—
with death a daily menace.

Mutinies threatened, there was
so little food. But Isaac
cached a bit he had from home
to keep hunger's claw at bay.
He pitied the plight of
less fortunate mates, "unspeakably
filthy wretches," who died a little more
each day while he lived in his frenzied head,
hearing poems fledge from privation.

Malignant spring bloomed noxious yellows
and pernicious weeds, while swearing officers
trimmed recruits. Soon only the few
fit were left. Ruddier and stronger now,
Isaac found himself unculled,
sent out to the King's Own
with more grub, better digs
and training—a battalion
formed of rugged moorland men
ticketed for France.

9. Leave-taking

Annie spoke through the high fence
in a low anxious voice as if afraid
to wake a fearful thing. She advised him
not to go, said he wasn't fit, but he

said otherwise. "I'll see the doctor,
and get you off," she soothed, but
Isaac said, "No, no." "Have you
any money?" she asked at last,
knowing he had none, and from her purse
poured out the little cash she had,
then, wordless, watched her brother turn and go.

Next day, to counter what was somber,
the boys marched down to the docks,
rasped voices raised in song:

We are the Bantam sodgers,
The short arse companee.
We have no height, we cannot fight.
What bloody good are we?

On the crossing, a damp
sea wind kept the Bantams sprawled
on deck awake. Yet, even
the most tired thought,
short as they were, they had the salt
to chase the Kaiser from Berlin.
Only Isaac was unsure. Even
a successful war
with its grotesqueries
might ruin Britain.

Riding a gentle tide, they moored
at Havre in fine weather
with larks and other songbirds
flitting, trilling, and twittering
in the skies and trees.

10. A Taste of War, June 1916

They went down to the trenches near Loos,
steel helmets heavy on their heads
and gas gear close at hand.

In a dugout cut into the muddy
wall, Isaac slept sitting up,
rats twining his ankles
or skittering over his hands.

By day, bullets buzzed close,
though raw wet weather
and blistered heels
proved a bigger bother.

Whether in or out of the line,
grub was the same—
Fray Bentos bully beef
and a swill of tepid tea—
less deadly than the barrage
or sporadic fire that killed two
and wounded twenty-three.
But lucky Isaac came through fine
this time, and with the unremitting rain
a torrent of poetry—
the visceral kiss of the real—
rushed like run-off
down a cold trench wall.

This current, so strong, needed
to be fed, pushing him to strip pages
from the Bibles of the dead.

Then suddenly, like a fresh sun,
new toil—salvage—exhumed him
to scavenge among ruined towns
for ammunition empties,
metal scraps, gas cans, and foil.

11. Back to the Front, August 1916

The fall fell heavily with wet and cold,
and then a light snow feathered down,
puffing white and deadly
out of a still sky. And Isaac
turned twenty-six as he marched

down to the Somme, the very place
where the womb of the world had ripped.

In a blasted universe, there seemed
nothing to believe in anymore,
though poetry, his Pegasus,
would never "lose or leave him."

A mere root sent freshly forth from Hades
to grip the sunless earth,
he wondered if yet another Jew
were destined to bear again
the sins of a capsized world.

Rain, snow, mud, and dirt was what
they knew now and hardly any cover.
Life intruded only in the scurried
movement of something fat and black—
the neutral rat, content to feed
on any flesh—Hun, Tommy, Poilu,
or Territorial, horse or mule.

Or it sufficed in lice.
"Better cold than lousy,"
he told himself, the insects
harder to defeat than other enemies—
a metaphor for war's futility
but grist for poems, a footing in the real
from which his Pegasus might soar.

His colonel declared him "hopeless"
at soldiering. And Isaac bounced about until
this errant shilling rolled into
the regimental kitchen, an assistant
battery cook working to defeat the Huns
with potato-peeling and cooking slop
over an open fire till
his khaki coat turned black.

But all the while poems peeled
out of him. He scratched

them onto scraps, whatever
he could pinch or pilfer
and puzzle together.
The war needed its Homer,
its Whitman, someone to make sense
of senseless things, to ring
humanity out of the dishrags.

Sent back to the work crew,
he fixed up pocked roads and rubbled
bridges, shuttled loads of wire
to the trenches in the pitchy night,
and brought back limber-carts of
the bloodied and the dead.

Then, on Christmas Day, no holiday for him,
the Jerries sent a biplane tumbling
from the clouds to strafe them,
the savior's day itself unsacred.

Spring brought rumors of another push,
some fresh shoots to be exhausted
beneath the sun's intrepid eye. But larks still sang
to greet him with the dawn
as he slogged back to camp
from a junket up the line,
his limber-cart hammering hard
over the stiffening bodies of new dead.

Between nightly forays
he made a stab at epic,
visioning the Amazonian
daughters of war keening
in the slow-whirling weird
to become the lovers of lost men.

12. First Leave, September 1917

Mimicking dragonflies, the Gothas
swarmed below the channel clouds

and hummed above London
to pitch bombs into his old haunts,
a shock to the homefolk.

Deloused and worried
for his mum, Isaac hurried
home in new duds
to find the family safe.

Feather light, though happy
and fitter than he'd ever been,
he loafed like Puck amid
the pubs and galleries,
an ash leaf floating on
the dullish pond
of dead civilian time.

Beneath the smiles and jokes,
he dreamt of unpregnant
goddesses and craved
the red rawness of life. Could not
Sonia have loved him
and lighted another way?
But that day too had passed.
Bereft of love, he left off
daydreams and longed now only
to get back into the fight.

13. To Arras, 1918

Influenza laid him low on his return
from leave. Two months in hospital
at Toul he languished in death's quiet lap,
two months free from the keening edge
of that other blade, scything
the grain near Cambrai.

Wheezily, he painted hurt boys
in runny watercolors
and read Lucretius on death,
a natural thing to face unfeared,

even as whizbangs hummed
and thundered overhead
and the dead stood upright
in unrolled razor wire.

There were rumors in the cutting wind, and the army needed
every *body* to plug some hole. So dear Isaac, flu-weak, was
sent down to the front to face deep winter in the greedy mud.

More useless than before, unfit for any job, he knew himself
a nuisance to the hardier and hale. He shivered
as a blizzard swirled out of frozen heaven and cursed
when freezing rains cut him to the skin and cold invaded every bone.

And then, as spring warmed its fingertips, rumblings came,
as if something untoward awaited, and Isaac
waited, too, feeling a sudden need to sit
with Solomon before the untouched temple wall
as the civil world began to topple and to burn,
flames spreading a rich new tapestry across the dirty sky.

Near Arras, he filed with a new battalion into the sodden trench.
And the big guns spoke their crazy talk, displaying rude bravado.
A thread, unraveling a little at each soft puff of breeze,
seemed all that held the chaos back.

                      And then one dawn, like almost any other,
the slim thread frayed, and the Jerries rolled in
as ineluctable as that morning's mist. The front line buckled,
and the tide washed right up to the last redoubt,
dragging bodies and blasted limbs to where Isaac
and his fellows lay, then broke and flooded back
bearing baubles in its hissing wake.

                            Afterward,
an unsilent silence deadened work, and heretofore unheard things
pulsed out, the solitary cries of the hurt,
the worried talk of the spared, more muffled orders,
the rhythmic click of accoutrements along the jagged trench line.

                            But soon enough
in the bleak distance, where the worsted land met sky,

a small thing began to swell as officers screamed retreat,
and Isaac cursed the power of a thing
so diademed in iron, lead, and surly fire.

14. The End

No one bothered to write the story,
so no one really knows or maybe ever knew.
It was a night sortie to Fampoux north
of the Somme, soon
after the Germans had swept forth
behind a curtain of fire and iron
and the hard-pressed Britons broke.

Ten died the night the boys probed north,
and Isaac lay out
with those few between the lines—
for twenty days prey
to birds and worse,
a somber nothing in his mind.

A hasty burial mixed his bones
with his messmates',
and none could later separate
Christian from Jew.

Book Seven

Envoi

1. Abdication and Exile, 1918

When his touring car, sans insignia,
puttered into Holland, he who had been
the sword and instrument of almighty *Gott*
had no plan or prospect. None knew he had come,
so he had no place to go. He surrendered
his sword of state to a bewildered border guard
and paced back and forth in the November cold
like a pouting child, a victim of himself.

Then a local someone, showing pity, brought
him to the coal-warm railway station, where he glumly
perched, a plucked chicken or odd imperial
bird, his stiff mustache already pointing toward
an obsolescence. Weeks before, in the faux
splendor of his Homburg spa, where he'd gone
"to take the cure," he had raised a proffered glass
of pale champagne, his face invested in its yellow
effervescence, offering a toast to Brest-
Litovsk, as if all future victories were won.

With the Russians out and no fool to make
him leery, he ordered all the flags run up in every
dusty burg, awarding, too, the worried kinder
a session off from school to temper them for war.

But when a final thrust west wilted on
the Somme, and Bolshies shot his whiskered cuz, he grew
distraught and distant. In a panic, he besought
to save his lifelong love, sweet Duchess Serge, a nurse
and nun, a solace to the soldiery of Russia.
But the Bolshies got her first and, mindful of
humanity, flung her down a mineshaft, casting
in a bomb or two to quell her daft hymn-singing.
Prophecies or premonitions? No one knows.
Kalkhas had gone missing.

                    But when Amiens fell
back to France, he fell too, prostrate with
a dizzy neuralgia, and his kingship lay abed
a whole day through, a helpless mustachioed child.

                                                            And yet,
next day, he rose, flush in the mild weather,
and dismissed gruffly the insolence of those
who said he should forego what had been but
the Almighty's to bestow. There was no one
to dream mountains of discarded crowns in the dacha
of the dead, so the Kaiser carried on
until the fleet defected and the army fled.

2. One Fine Day in Paris, 1918

Soon after the wreck and hush, there in the City
of Light, named for gas jets that once flickered
wickedly along the crowded boulevards,
a new age came striding in striped pants and morning
coat, doffing its high silk hat, a sour face
erupting in a toothy grin of victory.
Young girls smiled and strewed his path with peace-white roses
and the giddy *foules* broke out in boisterous cheers.

This bespectacled imperator had come,
without cross or scruple, to save a newer Rome.
But though he once had blinked in disbelief as Lee's
soldiers streamed barefoot by his gate, Wilson
was no Caesar. All war long he hunched safe
behind his sculptured desk, an ocean distant from
the mortal clash, while Kansas and New Jersey boys
bled and suffered—at least until the final German
gun was cast aside and the cannon's din
and deadly bluster calmed. And yet the victory
was his, this a new-made Enkidu, riding on
the bone-thin shoulders of the disappeared, arriving
now in glory to remold the European
world in ways Americans could not abide.

3. Blind Visions at Pasewalk, 1918

The Uecker River runs fast and true through lush, irenic
lakeland to lazy little Pasewalk where
in the quiet ward, another gas-blind no one

soaked in the sound of revolution, rumored strikes
and gossip, mutiny and defeat—and mused at what
his postwar fate might be, though it was plain
this painter couldn't see himself an artist anymore.

4. Requiescat

Washed in earth's damps or scoured
by rain, these ivory unsilences—
the testimony of Ors, Skyros, Koksijde or Calais—arrest all restless
rivers. Are they cursed or
blest, these million stillnesses provoked
by the petulance of leaves, by birdsong or by
the still unrisen
suns that might yet summon, out
of some strange recollection, the footsore wanderer
home to rest?

A threadbare thing renews itself, a bright
pulse more than quickened
in the race of life. Could it be
the fuse
eternal, the caress of
mind, the invisible touch of the lost?

A threadbare thing

Shall only death, then, speak of
life to those alive? Without this fecund loam, what would call us to
renew the threadbare khaki scratching at our elbows or wrest from
these living minutes a purpose beyond the wild thirst such
bodies, too, once knew?

A threadbare thing

Buried pathways veering
near lead us by
this same secret sorcery to a sunlit
spot among the lovely linden trees.

Hymns

To the Island of Philoctetes

Upon Reading Hassell's Life of Brooke in a Time of War

He came a yellow weed among
stone mullion and coign
and with skilled feet awoke
thunder-damp bone corridors
or shouted sonnets from beneath
the shadowy corbels,
a pearl called oyster, cascading
always after the belle and retroussé,
the smooth skin of youth
hiding a roughness
monstrous to itself.

Subjects studied: Latin, Greek,
limp scripture in a holy book.
Carlyle brought a dream of death:
Thrice stabbed, he comes
again a ghost to haunt
well-set Edwardian tables,
the gaunt, translucent dinner host,
chased by a mosquito.

Bored with the Arno's molten gold,
which poured serpentine through
Shelley's soulskin and out
over the pale green Tuscan-scape,
he turns from oils of Lucretia's
rape to the memory of lost women.

Where god's stripped out,
sucked dry or tombed,
a temporal human love becomes
the thing than which
there is none greater,
eternity's stuck in a ditch,
and heaven's blind.

[This space is left
for other items,
forgotten ones,
and wonderments—
the severed penises
of Hittites,
melted steel
of slow ships,
the sweat-stained
silks of young
Victorian women.]

The weave of the sky,
the juncture of
a million soon-to-be
forgotten things
sunken in a cask
or casket, trumps
the thighbone
of the deified:
All gods and kings
must be defied.

I saw a deep-tanned girl in Lancaster of late
working in the vegetable patch near the garden gate.
Tra-la!

And lifted light on the April breeze,
the songstress's voice among birch trees,
echoic on the river waves,
her thin lovely limbs
and fiery mane ablaze
in the lemony sun.
Tra-la!

And Taatamata, naked to the waist,
the straw hat broad and shadowing
a desuetude. Brown feet
covered over half in sugary
sand, giving beneath
the weight of words

a contrast to
the large orange
moon above
the lush lagoons
of Mataia.

Later he lay five days
in Greeley Square
awaiting conveyance
to Plymouth, dazed,
unready for the coquetry
of London life.

I turn a page,
and Brooke falls
out. There is some
staining on the flyleaf.
And like a scullion kitchen maid
who'd lost her lover, a robin runs
tunefully about the lawn
and calls beneath the shade
of whip-tower trees,
her russet front
a waistcoat made of
a loved brown leaf.

It came then, the vast shindy
of the war. Yes, Mrs. Cornford,
the sea and the pebbles seem
just the same, no evolution there—
unpaid-for cake, eyed from
beneath a tilted hat brim,
and the tea's gone cold,
yet every worthwhile thing is held
in the balance of a changeful gaze—
forthright—a raw eye
fixed on what must be opposed
at the cost of an ocean of blood.

Beside the slothful Cam
loquacious Brooke could

no longer burble on to friends
about a social cause and poems. He'd
seen the blackened corpses
sizzling in a rain of petrol
on the long march from Antwerp.

Indignant eyes safe for now over the tea table
learned nothing. Yes, for you, he wrote,
there is no change. For you,
the dead are just the silly dead.

Sand in My Pocket

Upon Reading Jones's Life of T. E. Hulme

1.

Walking back
beneath the shadowy
elms, Hulme
tucked under
one arm, I watch
my penumbra
slink along
the cement
and think:
*I wish
it could be
longer.*

Prince Ranier
      has died,
      so says
      the radio
      this morning,
      staticky voices
      released
      on ignition.
The car door
      slams out
      the first true
      day of spring.
The Pope lies
      in state.
I drive off
      safe from sunlight.

2.

Yesterday the bumblebees
      with humming wings

    assaulted the hanging
    white clusters of
    mountain laurel
    that grows unkempt
    beside the door.
But today the whorish bees
    have disappeared to spite
    the day's quiet brightness.
I sit in the sun
    that pours whitely
    through the wide
    mullioned window
    and read
    of T. E. Hulme.
I think: *words*
    do little
    to express
    simultaneousness
    as letter
    follows letter,
    word, word, so
    parataxis seems
    no ready method
    to capture being—Hulme,
T. E., was born
    at Gratton Hall,
    halfway between
    Hulme and Upper Hulme,
    a middle Hulmean he.

The rain has melted
    those Cambridge stones
    where he roomed
    near the Bridge of Sighs.
He talked philosophee
    the night through, a
    witty idler who declared
    no subject numinous,
and then was sent down in disgrace—
    the reason vague—an untoward
    something at the boat race,

    obstreperousness in the residence hall,
    a holy ruckus catcalling actors
    from the theater mezzanine.
    Maybe he had socked a cop
    during May week riots
    to celebrate the king's coming.
He left town astride
    a coffin in mock
    obsequies, proud
    in his derby hat.
To Canada he hied,
    traveling town to town
    pitching hay, lumberjacking,
    working in the timber mills
    to pay his way. He inclined
    toward the Roman Catholic
    as the huge Canadian sky
    and flat grassland that rolled
    away from his eye to the
    far horizon taught him
    the littleness of man. Art
    and the first gods, he reckoned,
    grew from fear.

Come home on a cargo boat,
    he poured the "bull-dust"
    of imagism down Pound's
    rust-rasped throat. Hulme
    thought the theory
    a kind of joke. I turn
    this over as my
    coffee cools. A bee—
    black carpenter—thunks
    twice against the pane,
    disturbing this reverie.
The American was earnest, eye
    on the ideal, the Brit
    ironic. To Hulme,
    Pound seemed a knot-head
    enthusiast who left
    Eliot seduced.

A blue-riven, sun-warmed April
        day seduces me
        from these browning
        pages and the dreams
        they bring. I plant
        beans and garlic
        and knock the ball
        around the yard
        a bit with Jared.
        The while I wonder
        why my friend—once
        Hulmean—has taken a
        Victorian turn—I've
        scorned it, so we move
        without seeming in
        opposite directions,
        as ships along the far
        horizon make way
        in phases imperceptibly.
Undersea, beyond eyeshot,
        small fish turn
        and whirl, part of
        a larger whole—
        imagism, vorticism.
        I belong
        to no school, but thrive
        on chaos—hoping
        for a scum-like
        rising, having learned
        that every particular
        view is wrong—the
        political stance is
        never
        to allow
        a political stance
        to shoulder the Kalashnikov.
Is man good
        and spoiled
        or limited and
        improved by order?
Hulme chose B. Hmm.

I hum bee-like inly
        as Jared presents
        tiny wildflowers
        white coronaed with
        a kind of bruised
        purple at the base—
a royal offering. He wants
        Vanilla Fingers
        and milk.

Hulme pensive: poetry
        could never move us
        beyond the physical.
True—though I hear
        a bird singing flute-like
        high in the oaks beyond
        this yard.

Unreliable words, he mused,
        tumbling apple-like
        out of the old farm cart,
        can estrange us usefully
        from the world. We feel
        afresh, wet, amniotic—
the true cry—a new physics.

Now the sun has gone away somehow,
        like Hulme's foot, lost
        in a camera quaver.
        Though the air stays mild,
the wind begins, rushing
        through unleaved high oaks
with the sound of a wild sea.
        At intervals it shapes
a violent tone—a threat
        of chaos that I like.

Hulme's logic locked him
        in a box. If the world's
a wind-up toy, we
        wound ourselves.

Why should anything exist?
This is the problem
of the materialist. Reason
sends itself
to the dustbin; isn't this
the postcard of
that other Hume?

So what if I'm just
    a kink in
    the winding sheet. Can
crickets think
    they can be other
    than they are
    and sing the same
    cheerful song?
Somehow I am always
    the houseguest at
    the Belvedere, listening
    to Raphael slap
    gaudy pigment
    on a wall.
My metaphor is showing
    its actory self
    in phony accents
    while I languish
    on the plum couch—
a sleeper—instant
    coffee in my cup.

T. E. says the symbol
    of the wheel
    is lost. But I am
watching the round
    wound
    on my thumb
    come from striking
    it on the doorjamb.

"Mana Aboda" rings
    metallic in my head

while songbirds lend
      a lilt to
           the strengthening sun. The kids'
           shouts ring too true
           as they play
           on the swing set
           and slide and in
           the sandbox. It
           won't always be
           like this. Diplodocus
           knew the sun
and warm, protecting sky,
      and Hulme, well-sexed,
with his Prussian face,
      is dead.
Shadows pool
      like oil leaked
      from the sun.
      On the verge of night
desire dreams continually of
      the furred pocket.
           Speech,
      ah!

For Wilfred Owen

Amid birdsong there are still
the pressures of the day,
the insistent telephone
and curt e-mail, a new
stain on the ceiling tile, while
out of doors the marigolds
are giving way to the rude
push of green.

I want to read
in Aeschylus of
the betrayal of brothers and something
of the short life of Owen,
but there are costs to pay.

The school insists
      amphetamines
for all the kinder,
      insists on nothing,
      having felt
      the pinch of
      a coming nothingness or
      the comingness of nonce.

A merry yellow face laughs,
      a buffoonish lemon drop on each
homework page, and every child's book
      seems chock to the top
      with princesses
      difficult to resist.
For Owen there was the war
      in every penstroke denoting
the motion of his hand and heartbeat
      under the grim din of guns.
For Aeschylus there was
      a brother cut to the quick as
the Persian host came on. Now,
      the world comes in a box

that flips all evil images
>		out, leaving but the fresh enticements of
a sugared green.

Singing from a Lower Branch

Upon Reading Hibberd's Life of Wilfred Owen

The reverberating black body of
the carpenter bee
hovering near
the rail leads me to wonder
what people were ever worth
a soldier's death.

With Owen I've heard
the Lord's word in
a Bible verse and
the effervescent bell calling me to serve,
even as the world swerves
away, beckoning for the nonce,
yet I've missed all consequential wars.

Rain with its million finger taps
upon the hollow roof makes it worse, signaling
thus softly: It is May in Eatontown, while later,
a blue jay, reprising his shrill song from the treetop,
calls back clear skies before falling down to
a lower branch on the twisted sycamore.

Bluebells, says the myth, fitted Owen
to poetry. He stitched his lines
in moonlight and eyed the master,
Swinburne, flitting through
meadow grass at Wimbledon.

The strange accident on Dunsden Green
gripped him with the fragility of things. Is
even to seek a new life to come
closer to the end? I see again the crumpled
service truck stuck between two tractor
trailers in Edison, the workman, in his dull blue shirt
and pants, pinned in, never having had
an inkling that morning over the shaving bowl
of his predicament, so the fated day

begins like any other, with a shower
and new underwear, though I recall
still the tan cloth-covered chairs in
the waiting room when my father got the news.

I'm waiting even now for Jared to come home from French
and thinking of Aeschylus who seemed to sense
God's helplessness. My daughter at three appears at stairtop, still
in her nightgown (light lavender), brown curls down
her back, just beginning the brief adventure,
a consciousness sucked open but a moment
to apprehend something in the otherwise void—where
planets cannot see the rush of comets trailing plumes
of glitter, or feel a star's heat, or hear the brash bump
of metaphors, nor understand salvation's bitter beat.

For Owen, talk of Christ was indigestible. He wavered
on the precipice and choked in the fetid air of
the savior's ancient tomb. Aiming instead, like a demon god's
dragoon, to send the earthly on,
he practiced shooting with his regiment
at Southport on the northwest shore, where once
I walked the boardwalk, a strange brass threepence in
a tiny hand, and hurt my feet at five on the pebbly strand
so unlike the sand-smooth beaches
at Spring Lake and Avon-by-the-Sea. And light,
too, seemed muted there like a dull picture,
or is this just how it is found now in memory?

Where does one find refreshment, since
every spring requires its sacrifices? Like the old
milkman in the frosty dawn of a cold school morning
rattling the bottles in the galvanized box
and waking up the household, we know it is coming.
And still, as if the milkman, bottles, box, and every morning
have not vanished in the daily magician's trick,
we each sit stuck in Parkway traffic like some timeless god,
blind whirling clocks for eyes.
                         In the *Iliad*, at least, the acute
waiting is all on the hero's part as the hoi polloi
deal death and die on the burning plain.

I awake, having dozed over this short life,
bathed in sweat on a lazy summer afternoon,
the killing sunlight a golden bullet slowly reaped, the light
and blinking eye soon merged, just as words
and what is written converge to codify a life.

Corpses lie, of course, like dung darkly lumped
through this landscape, though there were
summers when it seemed all summers
would be the same, feel the same, sound the same, with no
appreciable rushing.
                      "Have faith," I say, though
this morning I look like fifty. I've done heavy labor
in this field year on year—had I not
the gift then? As Gregg says, there is
really nothing to complain of, sitting on the
broad red veranda near the seaside, sipping
sharp martinis and sweet summer beer.

Reflections on Reflections

Reading a Life of Edward Thomas over Several Days in February

Earth enlisted him
in a shellburst
and took him to
its muddy mouth.

He doesn't even lie
in England so
can never be
the dust he loved—
soft under rain
in the barnyard.

On Fifth Avenue
this morning
there will be
rhythmed
a million
nobodies
and none
who've heard
this name,
so what
is war next
to the calamity
of writing?
The sun, not
quite soporific
before coffee,
filters through
the door shade,
but it is not to be
obeyed today.
It's cold—
and there's
a train—but
not to Adlestrop,
where it was June,

steam hissed,
and someone
cleared his throat,
though there could be
cloudlets floating in
the upper
atmosphere.

Though Thomas burned
poetry for cottage
fuel, his heart
lamented
the lost books
of childhood. His
mind whirled
with his mother's singing and
the melancholy smell of chalk.
He'd kept rabbits and pigeons in
the nannyless house, bricked in on every side,
and hoped notched petals of succory
might razor his throat or else daydreamed to drown
himself among river gulls and swans,
leaving nothing but the long gong of
the buoy bell in the sea off Wales.

He ran his hand along the bracken tops
and eyed the gorse flower and celandine.
Kissing and caressing and hidden away, he
took fresh Helen beneath the leaves
to make love on plush moss crosshatched in sunbeam.

They later lay—he and his Helen—with naked joy
beneath the deep-thatched cottage roof and breathed
the pussy musk and lover's dew and briar
roses that grew prickly up near benches on the porch.

The baby brought opium and beer—cheap rooms
and blacker moods—though the bells of a country
church still set him to writing in the Weald of Kent.
Watching the martins and chimney swifts feed
on the wing, he searched out their hidden nestings.

But the writing trade's a tough row, what with debt
and dishes mounting up and never a stop to it—
so youth's clean-limbed love brings long
troubles in train—
though one ought never
swap it for
a lesser thing.

His petulance scored
deliberate wounds
as love languished.
He wondered if acid Wiltshire rains
had soured this girl to womanhood, but she
proved stronger than he was strange,
cheerful as the celandine—petals freshly white against the frozen
February air. She minded the children while he wandered
through hayricks like the same cold wind that kept the roses blind.

A strong sunlight, such as he loved,
plays even now on planes of snow
striped purplish by the tall trunks of oaks
and sycamores on Sandspring. Maybe a wish
or simple opposition dials through
to summer nights when we lay down on clean,
heaped gravel, heads cradled in woven fingers
to appraise the stars pebbling the tarmac
of a long-dead sky, and saw a yellow meteor
streak, arc, and flash out of sight—so love
and discontent seem heaven-blent. What
is my emblem but a flower
that too quickly fades. The rain comes.
I fold my paintbox and go. His inner eye reprised
a childhood clouded with pigs clattering
down a rocky lane from a stone church and resaw
the bitter dahlias and sweet yellow apples eaten
under a pale sun. I remember the fresh
summer air of August evenings, the pink
sun dying in the West and how when it came
round again, I'd spring from the cooling sheets
to baseball in the sweet smelling grass—even
though I'd listened to the cricket shrieking

lonely near the damp basement wall
the whole night through.

He waited to be other than he was and knew
it would require thicker walking shoes. Neither he
nor almost anyone now knows how the fluid motion
of a dream informs the dust-bitten world
right down to its wet, chewed-off ends—
thoughts on other thoughts as Italian travelers
discuss destinations in the wood-warm station.
At Little Silver I await the 10:52, Thomas's
life open on my lap. I find he wished
to oscillate between violet and rose,
to be a thing as sugar-tossed and suited to its place
as harebell and snowdrop—and like as thoughtless.

His dream dissolved, he clung to something hard about himself
that he might polish up to something. Then,
when the war was on, there were picnics still at Ryton
with long rambles through Lord Beauchamp's fields
and forests with Frost and Abercrombie, Brooke and Gibson, too.

I'm tired of dappled leaves, but not your profile, young complected
as you muse over something you've just read in a book that seems
serious, and for a moment I long to see you in nothing but your socks.
You have a long and longing thigh, lady, beneath
your pinstriped trouser leg, one slung lazily over
the other and jogging with the rhythm of the train,
and likely a tart tongue, too, though your lips seem
gentle enough and softly pink.

He looked for sun nymphs and words to rise
out of the grave, a-chanting with salty gusto.
And there one arises, copper-haired
in a red sweat jacket and earphones,
a slight dampness under the arms,
and even that lovely—oh, no plot so
narrow but be nature there. I read:

Frost and he got snooty when
the gamekeeper warned them off—

oh, take the one less traveled by.
I recall how lovely shined
the coffee-colored mud the snowmelt
made on the pavement near
the New York Public Libraree,
feet slapping in the muck, like
fallen leaves, their ruddy music,
while Thomas's manuscripts lie
moldering in the temple of books
with other soft forgotten things.

He thought a beezer full of dirt
might remedy all. But this I know:
thwarted hope has a sharp edge.

I too wish I could stop this flow,
remembering my grandmother,
her pillbox hat and veil
stultified against a pale blue wall,
everything frozen over for Easter
morning to begin. We leave
for the little white church
and come home feeling saved,
though it's a tick or two later
on the trip to oblivion.

Thomas watched farm toughs
pitch corn by the wagonload but never
pitched in. Sometimes I think
I might like to do some country work,
scythe the whispering hay in the pleasant
September sun, watching hoppers
jump and catch the light in their
lucent wings, or heap hay up
five feet beyond the wagon top.

Near 10th I'm thinking I've walked
this street a hundred times and
outwalked a vital thing before
I knew it. The last time
I heard Bu was at Sweet Basil, where

soft brushwork bled to silence
all through "It Might as Well
Be Spring." He died that year.
Later that same night we
ducked into the basement
at the 55, where Greg
Hutchinson's brushes lisped
over an old snare.

He was just
a kid then
with his
hat reversed.

I notice this time
how Empire
Szechuan rumbles with
underpassing subway
trains. The
short martini wavers
in a stemmed glass
giving different images
of olives. I look
again at Helen's
picture, an etched-
over photograph—
her hair parted, neat, and
eyes forthright.
There is a kind
of loveliness about
the lips. Of all
the books I could
have read . . . I wonder,
couldn't he
have loved
her more
than his other
longing? Soon
there is roast duck
in black bean sauce
and a bowl of

bleachy rice. 4:30.
I wonder too how
the waitress,
who never heard
of Absolut, knew
to come to New
York. There
are just me
and three older women,
all at separate tables—
and they
seem pleasant
enough,
though I
can't imagine what
they're reading.

Struck from the Chill of the World

Upon Reading J. M. Wilson's Life of Isaac Rosenberg

1.

Were you here with me, Isaac,
        in this quiet room on Sandspring
this rainy August afternoon, how alien
        would we be, one to another? Would
you be wearing your thick wool
        tunic or, dismissed and jobless,
peer at me from beneath
        your fedora's brim with sardonic eyes
meant to conceal a shyness?

        It's a modern conceit,
a century aged in opposition to
        reticent stars, which cast
their yellow eyelashes down upon
        the dark lucidity of a lost lake.

Death, of course, makes
        a momentary catch in the breath,
postponing the refreshment of dreams. But
        your Jewishness
or Britishness would be no barrier,
        as each has folded me into itself
with loving arms.
        And yet I wonder:
How could it have been so long?

2.

Silas in the next yard sings
        "when the dog bites, when
the bee stings" and like
        one of Crane's urchins
gaily digs in dust

        and loam, though
there is no nearby
        bottom of the sea
to prove so cruel. I lay your life
        open on my lap
to listen for a spell,
        hoping this boy, so beautiful,
will find a kinder world
        than heartless fates allowed to you.

Once a boy as young,
        I may have known some vets
from your war, having
        watched a dozen march
all out of step through Asbury
        in their still smart olive drabs,
none worse for wear. Do I remember still
        a tear pearling? Was it pity
or pride as those men, so scarred
        with suffering, passed by
and forever out of
        my living life? One hobbled
a little, yet still strode boldly,
        his varnished cane fixing
him in line as the ruffed drums
        drove them all on in time.
But these were Americans.

3.

My great granddad William,
        a painter and engraver, too,
a soldier in Salonika, was still
        alive then though far away
on Broadgate near the Ribble. We never
        came face to face or shared
a word between us.
        No one thought to bear
the long-distance cost, though now
        his painting shares this space,

hanging in its drift of silence—
        decidua of a life lived.

4.

For you, costs abruptly busted in,
        and peacetime Britain could find no way
to use you, so skilled and bright.
        So, she offered you up,
death's votary. I'm
        remembering now
two jays—suburban Poilu shrieking
        in the lilac bush, soon
winging off to chase a crow
        that had been busy
caching a speckled egg
        in the thickened summer grass,
the fruits of theft abandoned like
        the blind eye of the lawn.

5.

Never one to love your ignorance,
you studied Herbert and Donne, folding them
into your leaven so you might not become
another's parakeet, might brave
that first great decadent age, wielding
a fought-for eloquence wrested from stammers.

The breeze comes quiet this May morning,
just cool enough for neighbors to sit
out in secluded yards scanning the news,
sipping bitter coffee, resisting the day, while
in the dead limb of a distant oak, the woodpecker
exhales its melancholy cry.

Notes

Book One: Invocations and Insistencies

Gavrilo Princip (1894–1918): A Bosnian Serb who assassinated both the Austrian Archduke Franz Ferdinand and the archduke's wife, Sophie, on Franz Joseph Street in Sarajevo. He was tried, found guilty, and imprisoned in the Terezin fortress.

Kalkhas: Greek augur who, when the Greek fleet was becalmed at Aulis, prophesied that Agamemnon would have to sacrifice his daughter Iphigenia in order to gain a favorable wind to carry the army to Troy. When, in the tenth year of the Trojan War, Apollo afflicted the Greek army with plague, Kalkhas prophesied that to lift the plague, Agamemnon would have to return his captive lover Khryseis to her father.

Milos Obilic: Legendary fourteenth-century Serbian knight said to have assassinated the Turkish sultan.

"I hear the singing of a saw on bone": Princip suffered from tuberculosis while imprisoned. The disease affected his bones, and he had to have his right arm amputated. But the line also refers to a comment Confederate General Thomas J. "Stonewall" Jackson made while his arm was being amputated after the Battle of Chancellorsville.

kmets: Serfs in the Balkans.

zadrugas: South Slavic rural communities.

Todor Princip: An early nineteenth-century headman of the Princip family.

Book Two: Rupert Brooke

Ka: Katherine Laird Cox (1887–1936), a Fabian, Neo-Pagan graduate of Newnham College, Cambridge University. She met Brooke at Cambridge, and the two became lovers in 1911. Although they broke up in 1912, they continued to correspond even after Brooke's enlistment in 1914.

Philoctetes: Greek hero of the Trojan War and the subject of a number of plays in classical times, the most notable of which is that by Sophocles, the only one extant. Philoctetes was the most expert archer among the Greeks. He had inherited the bow of Heracles and was the only person who was able to use it. On the way to Troy, the Greek fleet stopped at the island of Tenedos, where a snake bit Philoctetes on the foot. By some accounts, the wound festered and gave off an offensive smell that caused the Greeks to leave him stranded on the island of Lemnos. After the death of Achilles, the Greeks realized that they could not take Troy without the use of the bow of Heracles and that the bow was useless without the one man who had mastered it. In the *Trojan Epic* by Quintus of Smyrna, Agamemnon sends Odysseus and Achilles' son Neoptolemus to Lemnos to bring back Philoctetes and the bow. In the *Little Iliad*, Diomedes performs this service. In his famous work of literary criticism, Edmund Wilson used the myth of Philoctetes to posit that the well-springs of imaginative writing (the artist's bow) are the psychic wounds the writer has received, generally in childhood.

Fabians: The Fabian Society was a British socialist organization formed in 1884, to which Brooke and many of his friends belonged. The Fabians promoted pacifism.

Edward Marsh (1872–1953): Friend and patron of Rupert Brooke, Siegfried Sassoon, and Isaac Rosenberg, among others. He was the editor of the anthology *Georgian Poetry*, which introduced new poetry to the British public. During the war, he served as secretary to First Lord of the Admiralty Winston Churchill.

Ansons: The battalion of the 63rd Naval Division in which Brooke served. It was named for eighteenth-century British Admiral George Anson.

Cathleen: Cathleen Nesbitt (1888–1982), Irish actress who became Rupert Brooke's lover in 1912. Nesbitt went on to appear in many stage, film, and television productions, including the Broadway show *My Fair Lady* in 1956 and the television programs *Dr. Kildare* and *Upstairs, Downstairs*.

Leto: One of the female Titans of Greek mythology and the mother by Zeus of Apollo and Artemis.

Laurette's song: "Peg o' My Heart," popularized by the American actress Laurette Taylor.

Petrushka: Ballet by Igor Stravinsky starring Vaslav Nijinsky, which was staged in London at the Drury Lane Theatre in 1914.

Drury Lane: The Theatre Royal in London's West End, built in 1812.

Mataia: An area of Tahiti near the beach where Brooke lived during the early part of 1915.

Taatamata: Beautiful native Tahitian woman who became Brooke's lover in 1915. Although Brooke thought she had died soon after he left the island, she lived into the 1930s and may have borne Brooke a daughter.

Byron's pool: The weir pool in Grantchester, England, where Lord Byron used to swim, now a local nature reserve.

Gallipoli: A peninsula of European Turkey that juts into the Aegean Sea. The Hellespont and the strait of the Dardanelles separate it from Asia Minor. The battle that takes its name from the peninsula raged around it from 17 February 1915 to 9 January 1916. More than 100,000 British, French, and Turkish soldiers perished during the campaign.

Book Three: T. E. Hulme

Ezra Pound (1885–1972), American poet and theorist. After spending some months in Spain and Italy, the Idaho-born Pound settled in London in 1908. By 1909, he had entered Hulme's modernist literary circle.

Kate: Kate Lechmere (1887–1976): British artist and co-founder with Wyndham Lewis of the Rebel Art Centre, London, in early 1914. Lewis and Lechmere were also romantically involved at this time. Lewis brought Hulme to the Rebel Art Centre that spring, where the latter made the acquaintance of Lechmere and supplanted Lewis as her lover. The jealous Lewis, vowing to kill Hulme, famously stormed into Dolly Kibblewhite's salon and assaulted Hulme there.

The fight spilled down the stairs and out into Soho square, where Lewis tried to strangle Hulme. But Hulme, much the larger and stronger of the two, soon broke free, turned Lewis upside down, and hung him by his pants cuffs from a tall wrought-iron fence.

Wyndham Lewis (1882–1957): Novelist, painter, and critic, and co-founder of the Vorticist movement in art and of the Rebel Art Centre. He was Kate Lechmere's lover before Hulme.

Rebel Art Centre at 38 Great Ormond Street, London: A meeting place, exhibition space, and lecture room dedicated to non-representational and geometric art. Henri Gaudier-Brzeska exhibited his sculpture at the center, and Ezra Pound lectured there. It opened in January 1914 and closed for good that summer.

Mrs. Kibblewhite: The artist Ethel "Dolly" Kibblewhite, née Curtis (1873–1947). She had studied art at the Slade School. In 1911, she became a close friend and lover to Hulme. She held a salon for artists and writers at her home at 67 Frith Street, where Hulme became the dominant figure.

Kenneth Powell (1885–1915): British tennis player who participated in the 1908 and 1912 Olympics and played a number of years at Wimbledon.

Ajax: One of two Greek heroes of the Trojan War by that name, considered to be the largest and the strongest man in the Greek army and the best warrior after Achilles.

Gratton: Hulme was born at Gratton Hall, Endon, Staffordshire.

St. Eloi: The French name for the Belgian village of Sint-Elooi in Flanders. Fighting raged around St. Eloi throughout much of the spring of 1915.

Café Royal: Cafe in the hotel at 68 Regent Street in the Piccadilly section of London.

Henri Gaudier-Brzeska (1891–1915): French-born artist and sculptor. He moved to London in 1910 and became one of the Vorticist (abstractionist) group. As such, he was closely associated with T. E.

Hulme, Ezra Pound, and Wyndham Lewis. He sculpted a bust of Pound and crafted Hulme's famous knuckleduster.

Bertrand Russell (1872–1970): British philosopher and prominent pacifist during World War I. He and Hulme publicly disputed whether the war was just and necessary.

Robert Bevan (1865–1925): British painter who was one of the first in England to experiment with Fauvism.

Richard Curle (1883–1968): Scottish literary critic and writer and, beginning in 1912, a member of the novelist Joseph Conrad's circle.

C. R. W. Nevinson (1889–1946): English artist who studied at the Slade where he befriended Isaac Rosenberg. He was also a close friend of Wyndham Lewis and a member of his Rebel Art Centre. During the war, he served in the Friends' Ambulance Unit and the Royal Medical Corps. In his own art, Nevinson adopted the Futurist style, after having met the Italian artist Filippo Marinetti.

Ramiro de Maeztu (1875–1936): Spanish essayist and journalist who served as the London correspondent for a number of Spanish newspapers.

Cromarty: Small fishing village on the south shore of the mouth of Cromarty Firth in the Highlands of eastern Scotland. At the beginning of the twenty-first century, the population was 719. The firth was used as a naval base during the war.

Jacob Epstein (1880–1958): New York-born sculptor who moved to London in 1905 and became a British subject. He and Hulme became close friends, and Hulme wrote glowingly about Epstein's work, particularly the Vorticist sculpture *Rock Drill*. In an essay in *Sketch* magazine, Hulme pronounced Epstein "the greatest sculptor in England today." Epstein sculpted a portrait head of Hulme and wrote the preface for Hulme's posthumously published book of essays on humanism and art. During the war, Epstein served in the Jewish Legion of the British Army.

Nieuport Bains: Bathing resort on the Belgian coast, near the city of Nieuport.

Passchendaele: Fought between July and November 1917, Passchendaele was the third of five battles between British and German imperial forces for control the city of Ypres, Belgium. In the end, the British failed to capture the city, though they pushed the German line back, gains that were shortly given up. The only real advantage for the allies was that the campaign diverted German men and materiel away from the southern front where the French army was hard-pressed. Casualties (killed, wounded, and missing) differ, but a reasonable estimate is the British suffered 275,000 and the Germans 225,000. About 70,000 British soldiers were killed. British Prime Minister Lloyd George later wrote that Passchendaele was a "senseless campaign."

Common Prayer: The Book of Common Prayer is the liturgical book used in the Anglican and Episcopal churches. It includes prescribed prayers for different purposes as well as standard ceremonial scripts for different religious occasions, including marriage, burial, and Christian holidays.

Book Four: Wilfred Owen

Fairie Queene: Long sixteenth-century poem written by Edmund Spenser.

Willmer Road: The Owens briefly lived at 14 Willmer Road, Birkenhead, when Wilfred was about six years old.

"holiest bard": Samuel Taylor Coleridge lived for a time at Greta Hall, Keswick.

Vivian Rampton: Twelve-year-old son of a Dunsden bricklayer with whom Owen seems to have had an early infatuation and to whom he gave secret piano lessons.

Milly Montague: Twelve-year-old Dunsden girl with whom Owen became friendly.

Dunsden Green: Village in South Oxfordshire where Owen was assistant to the parish priest.

Raymond Poincaré (1860–1934): President of France from 1913 to 1920.

Henriette Poitu: Sixteen-year-old beauty whom Owen met during his sojourn in Bordeaux.

Russell Square: A large garden square in the Bloomsbury section of London.

Escoula's music: Jean Escoula's sculpture of *La Muse Bagnéraise* in la Place des Thermes in Bagnéres. A verse by Owen's friend Laurent Tailhade is inscribed on the back of the plinth.

Théophile Gautier (1811–1872): French poet, dramatist, and novelist widely admired by modernists.

Mme. Charles Léger: Wife of a French elocution teacher. Wilfred tutored her in English during his time in Bordeaux.

Laurent Tailhade (1854–1919): French poet of Bagnéres who befriended Owen.

Birkenhead: Town in Cheshire where the Owen family lived from 1900 to 1907. Wilfred Owen attended the Birkenhead Institute for part of his education.

Anatole France (1844–1924): French poet and novelist who was awarded the Nobel Prize for Literature in 1921.

Artists Rifles: A volunteer regiment of the British Army formed in 1859 that recruited many artists, writers, and other creative men.

Dulce et decorum est pro patria mori ("Sweet and fitting it is to die for one's country"): A line from the Roman poet Horace.

Mars: Roman god of war.

Minerva: Roman goddess of wisdom, weaving, music, and war.

Loos: A battle on the western front during which the British attempted to capture Artois and Champagne from the Germans. It took place from 25 September to 8 October 1915 and represented the major British offensive operation on the western front that year. The British suffered 8,000 casualties in the first four hours of the battle. Overall, British casualties in the Battle of Loos amounted to 59,247 with more than 20,000 killed, including Rudyard Kipling's only son, John. The Germans suffered some 26,000 killed, wounded, and missing.

Bloomsbury: A district in London's West End associated with art and literature. It was home to the Bloomsbury group's most famous member, Virginia Woolf. Yeats also lived there.

William Butler Yeats (1865–1939): Irish writer who is widely considered to be the finest poet to write in English in the late nineteenth and early twentieth centuries. He won the Nobel Prize for Literature in 1923.

Harold Monro (1879–1932): Belgian-born English poet and proprietor of the Poetry Bookshop at 35 Devonshire Street in Bloomsbury. The shop became a center for Georgian and modern poetry.

Alida Klemantaski (1892–1969): Monro's assistant at the Poetry Bookshop and later his wife. She was an author and editor in her own right.

Rabindranath Tagore (1861–1941): Bengali poet, philosopher, and artist.

Romford: Town in East London where the 2nd Battalion of Artists Rifles was stationed for training.

Herbert Briggs: Nineteen-year-old volunteer in the Artists Rifles and subsequently a friend of Owen.

Hampstead Heath: A hilly nature reserve north of London between Highgate and Hampstead.

John Keats (1795–1821): One of the greatest English poets. Keats died young as a result of tuberculosis. He lived in Hampstead at the end of his life before going to Italy in an attempt to regain his health. He died in Rome.

Somme: River in Picardy, France, which gave its name to the battle that took place along its banks from 1 July to 18 November 1916. Ironically, the name means "tranquility." The Battle of the Somme was one of the most horrific in history. The British and French suffered some 485,000 casualties and the Germans about 630,000. More than 125,000 British and imperial troops were killed, including 20,000 in the first hour of fighting.

Calais: Major port city in northern France through which much traffic to and from England passes.

Hogmanay: The Scottish New Year celebration.

Crécy: A battle of the Hundred Years' War between France and England. It took place in northern France in 1346 and resulted in an English victory, partly because the longbow arrows of the English archers could pierce French armor.

Amiens: City in northern France through which the River Somme runs. It is home to Amiens Cathedral, the largest church in France. The city was heavily damaged in the war.

Bouchoir: Village in northern France about twenty-two miles southwest of Amiens.

Punch: British weekly humor magazine founded in 1841.

Elizabeth Barrett Browning (1806–1861): Victorian English poet best known for her *Sonnets from the Portuguese*. She was the wife of the poet Robert Browning.

Alexander the Great (356–323 BCE): Macedonian general and king who conquered Greece, Egypt, the Middle East, and part of India.

Selency: Small French village near St. Quentin.

Lt. Arthur Heydon: Owen's immediate superior in Company A of the 2nd Manchester regiment. In civilian life, he had been an accountant in Stockport. He had been wounded at Gallipoli.

St. Quentin: A small city in northern France that was much fought over in World War I. The Germans captured and looted it in 1914 and later incorporated it into the Hindenburg Line. By war's end, most of the city was destroyed.

Beauvois; Small village in northern France about thirty miles northwest of Arras.

Arras: Capital of the Pas-de-Calais department in northern France. Arras was heavily damaged during World War I, with heavy fighting nearby during 1914, 1917, and 1918.

Mary Millard Owen (1896–1956): Wilfred Owen's sister.

Savy Wood: A staging area for British troops near St. Quentin.

Gaia: The primordial Earth goddess in ancient Greek mythology. She was the wife of Uranus and the mother of Chronos and Rhea.

2nd Lt. Hubert Gaukroger (1885–1917): An officer in Company B of the 2nd Manchester Regiment. He was killed in the fighting near St. Quentin in April 1917.

Capt. Sebastian Sorrell (1891–1953): Commander of Company B of the 2nd Manchester Regiment. Like Owen, Sorrell wrote poetry. He was also sent home to England after suffering shellshock.

Dr. William Brown: The senior neurologist at the Casualty Clearing Station at Gailly, where Owen was sent after having been blown up at Savy Wood in April 1917.

Craiglockhart: A former hydropathic hotel near Edinburgh that was converted into an official war hospital for neurasthenic officers in 1916.

Dr. Arthur Brock: Medical doctor and sociologist who oversaw Owen's treatment at Craiglockhart.

pararhyme: A half-rhyme that changes the vowel sound but preserves the same consonant pattern.

Siegfried Sassoon (1886–1967): English poet and decorated officer in World War I who met Owen at Craiglockhart and helped him to modernize and improve his poetry.

Uranians: A secret group of gay poets, chiefly English, who were active from the 1850s to the 1930s, among whom Sassoon included himself.

"Anthem": Owen's great poem "Anthem for Doomed Youth," written in 1917.

Oscar Wilde (1854–1900): Famed Irish playwright and novelist who spent two years at hard labor in prison after conviction for "gross indecency" with men.

Robert Ross (1869–1918): Canadian-born art critic, dealer, and journalist. He was a longtime friend and perhaps sometime lover of Oscar Wilde and became his literary executor.

H. G. Wells (1866–1946): English writer notable for his novels *The Time Machine*, *The Invisible Man*, and *The War of the Worlds*.

The Nation: British radical weekly newspaper.

Robert Graves (1895–1985): British poet, novelist, and critic, and friend of Sassoon. He served as an officer in the Royal Welch Fusiliers and was badly wounded at the Battle of the Somme.

Southport: Seaside resort town in Lancashire, England.

Germaine: Town in the Marne department of northern France.

Serre-lès-Puiseaux: Village in northern France, which the Germans seized early in the war. The allies recovered it in early 1917 only to lose it again the next year.

"Unimagined things": The phrase comes from Gregg Glory's line "Unimagined things grow real, grow real" from his poem "Unimagined Things."

Capt. Hugh Somerville: Commanding officer of D Company of the 2nd Manchesters, in which Owen served. He was wounded at Joncourt in early October 1918.

Jones: The son of a Herefordshire gardener, he was Wilfred Owen's servant during much of his military service. Historians have been unsuccessful in discovering his given name or what happened to him after his wounding.

Oise-Sambre Canal: The canal that connects the Sambre and Oise rivers near the small village of Ors in northern France.

Hancourt: Small village in northern France just east of the River Somme.

Algernon Swinburne (1837–1909): English poet who was greatly influential among young poets between 1890 and World War I. Interest in his work began to fade with the advent of modernism, which eschewed Swinburne's florid style. He took on controversial topics, including lesbianism, cannibalism, atheism, and sado-masochism.

"He won his cross": The Military Cross, bestowed only on commissioned officers, was the second highest decoration given during World War I. It was awarded for "exemplary gallantry." In the context of the poem, though, the word "cross" also carries the connotation of a burden as well as of sacrifice in a religious sense.

Houghmond Hill: Wooded hill in Shropshire where Owen used to ramble prior to the war.

Styx: In Greek myth, the river that separates the upper earth from the underworld and the living from the dead, though the living sometimes visited the underworld of Hades.

Book Five: Edward Thomas

"da Vinci's vision": In his notebook, Leonardo da Vinci drew a picture of a chain-driven, pedaled bicycle. This idea, however, bore no immediate fruit. Forms of two-wheeled bicycles first came into use in the early nineteenth century, but the chain-driven variety was not produced until 1885.

Ryton: A small village in Gloucestershire.

Robert Frost (1874–1963): American poet whose works were first published in England.

Artemis: In Greek mythology, she is the goddess of the hunt, the moon, the wilderness, wild animals, and chastity.

Coventry: City in central England near Birmingham, notable for its cathedral.

Steep Station: Rail station near where Thomas lived in the village of Steep, Hampshire.

High Beech: Helen and the children moved to High Beech, Essex, eleven miles from London, after Thomas joined the army.

Myfanwy Thomas (1910–2005): Daughter of Edward and Helen Thomas.

Mona's Queen: Side-paddle-wheel steamer that served during the war to transport British troops to France.

Neuve-Chapelle: Small village in northern France near Calais.

Mondicourt: Farm village near Calais.

Ludcombe: Small cottage the Thomas family inhabited in Epping Forest during the war, also spelled Lutcombe.

estaminets: Small cafés in France that sell alcoholic drinks.

Beaurains: A town three miles south of Arras, France.

Achicourt: A suburb of Arras, France.

Epping Forest: Ancient woodland in Essex, England, where the Thomas family lived during the war.

Book Six: Isaac Rosenberg

Bristol: A major commercial city in southwestern England where Rosenberg was born. Coleridge lived in Bristol in 1795.

"unlikely bride": Coleridge married the Bristol-born Sara Fricker in 1795, reputedly because he needed a wife with whom to begin the cooperative Pantisocratic society he and Robert Southey had planned. Coleridge later deemed he and his wife to be incompatible temperamentally and did not believe her to be in tune with his creative endeavors nor sympathetic to his literary associates. But he and Sara, though estranged, remained married until his death.

T. S. Eliot (1888–1965): American ex-patriot poet who with his poem "The Waste Land" became the key figure in the early modernist movement.

East End: The overcrowded and impoverished district of London where many Jewish immigrants lived by the turn of the twentieth century.

Sonia Cohen: A young sweatshop worker with whom Rosenberg became infatuated after meeting her in the Whitechapel Library. He painted an oil portrait of her. She later wrote a memoir.

David Bomberg (1890–1957): British painter who attended the Slade with Rosenberg.

Cyrano de Bergerac: The character in Edmond Rostand's play of the same name. De Bergerac proves too shy to approach the woman he loves because he is self-conscious of his appearance. He compensates vicariously by penning letters for another of her lovers, one who lacks de Bergerac's facility with words.

Mrs. Herbert Cohen: Mrs. Cohen, known for her philanthropy, paid Rosenberg's tuition to the Slade for his first year, but he soon found her to be too meddlesome in his private affairs and dispensed with her backing.

The Slade: Slade School of Art, London, founded in 1868, perhaps the most prestigious art school in England.

Whitechapel: A section of the East End, London, and home to the "Whitechapel Boys," a predominantly Jewish avant-garde art and literary movement.

Mark Gertler (1891–1939): A London-born Jewish artist who attended the Slade with Rosenberg.

Lady Diana Manners (1892–1986): Although she was officially the daughter of the duke and duchess of Rutland, she was in reality the duchess's illegitimate daughter by the writer Henry Cort. She was widely considered the most beautiful woman in England. She attended the Slade with Rosenberg but did not pursue a career in the arts. She later married Duff Cooper, the British ambassador to France, who was created Viscount Norwich, at which point she became a viscountess.

Dora Carrington (1893–1932): British artist who attended the Slade with Rosenberg and later became part of the Bloomsbury group through her close association with Lytton Strachey. She committed suicide in 1932 after Strachey's death.

Phyllis Gardner (1890–1939): Writer, artist, and, as only recently discovered, lover of Rupert Brooke. She attended the Slade with Rosenberg.

Ernest Dowson (1867–1900): An English poet, fiction writer, and translator. With Yeats, he had been a member of the Rhymers' Club.

Max Beerbohm (1872–1956): English essayist, humorist, and caricaturist.

George Bernard Shaw (1856–1950): Irish playwright and famed socialist.

Roger Fry (1866–1934): English artist, art critic, and translator of Mallarmé, who associated with the Bloomsbury group in London. He was the curator of painting at the Metropolitan Museum of Art in New York before World War I. Fry was the first to use the word "Post-Impressionism."

Laurence Binyon (1869–1943): English poet and translator, chiefly known today for his poem "For the Fallen," written in memory of Britain's war dead. The "Ode of Remembrance" section of the poem is often read at World War I memorial ceremonies.

Domino Room: This room on the lower floor of the Café Royal in London with its mirrors and gilding was the haunt of artists and writers in the late 1800s and early twentieth century.

Minnie (Rosenberg) Horvitch (b. 1883): Isaac's older sister, who moved to South Africa after her marriage.

Marda Vanne: The later stage name of Margueretha van Hulsteyn, with whom Rosenberg had a brief fling during his time in Cape Town. He drew her portrait, and she inspired him to write some passionate love poems.

Elizabeth Molteno (1852–1927): The well-to-do daughter of the Cape Colony's first prime minister. She put Rosenberg up at her luxurious home in Cape Town during part of his stay. She was a civil rights activist and feminist.

Meshuggah: The Yiddish word for "crazy."

Mons: City in Belgium near where the battle of the same name was fought in August 1914. The British suffered 1,600 casualties but inflicted some 5,000 on the Germans. For these reasons, the British declared it a victory even though they were ultimately forced to retreat.

Marne: The battle along the Marne River in France from 6 to 12 September 1914 began with a French/British counterattack that succeeded in pushing the Germans back from Paris. The French and British casualties amounted to 263,000 with 80,000 French and 1,700 British killed. The Germans lost 67,000 men.

Ypres: A battle fought around the Belgian town of Ypres from 19 October to 22 November 1914 that was largely a stalemate, though all involved, including the Belgians, French, British, and Germans suffered heavy casualties.

Boer War: War fought from 1899 to 1902 between the British Empire and the independent Boer states of South Africa. The Boers were the descendants of Dutch settlers of the Cape of Good Hope. The British ended up taking over South Africa.

Absalom: The son of Israel's King David. He was said to have been the handsomest man in the kingdom. He ultimately revolted against his father in a bid to seize power and was killed.

Suffolks: The Suffolk Regiment, which Rosenberg joined in 1915.

Annie Rosenberg (1892–1961): Isaac's sister.

Lillers: Town in northern France near Calais.

Lières: A small village near Calais.

Fray Bentos: Canned corned beef supplied to British troops by Liebig's Extract of Meat Co. It was named after the town in Uruguay where the company had its factory. The phrase "Fray Bentos" became slang for "good" among the troops.

Pegasus: Famous winged horse of Greek mythology.

Walt Whitman (1819–1892): American poet credited with discovering a new form and idiom for American poetry. Rosenberg considered him to be the Homer of the American Civil War.

"Amazonian daughters": The Amazons were fierce female warriors of Greek mythology. In his poem "Daughters of War," Rosenberg imagined these Amazons wailing for their mortal lovers to die and come to them. He may have thought to compose an epic about World War I from this poem or its theme.

Gothas: Heavy biplane bombers used by the *Luftstreitkräfte* during World War I.

Cambrai: Town on the Scheldt River in northeastern France. It was occupied by the Germans from 1914 until 1918. The Battle of Cambrai, which featured the first substantial use of tanks, took place near the town in late 1917.

Lucretius: Roman Epicurean poet of the first century BCE.

Solomon: Tenth-century BCE king of Israel, noted for wisdom. He was the builder of the first temple in Jerusalem, a poet and prophet, and the last ruler of a united Israel.

Book Seven: Envoi

Brest-Litovsk: A peace treaty Germany signed in 1918 with the new Bolshevik regime in Russia. It took Russia out of the war and allowed the Germans to concentrate on the Western Front.

"Whiskered cuz": Tsar Nicholas II.

Grand Duchess Serge (1864–1918): Kaiser Wilhelm II's cousin Elisabeth of Hesse and by Rhine. She was a granddaughter of Queen Victoria. Wilhelm became infatuated with her in the 1870s when he was a student in Bonn. He wrote poems to her and proposed marriage, but she rejected his proposal and later married Grand Duke Sergei of Russia. After the duke's murder in 1905, she became a nun. Wilhelm always retained his love for her. The Bolsheviks murdered her in 1918.

"King Billy Bomb Balls": The phrase is from W. B. Yeats's poem "Lapis Lazuli" and alludes to the bombs Zeppelins dropped on England during World War I.

Pasewalk: Town in northeastern Germany where a military hospital was located. Adolph Hitler was treated for temporary blindness there after being wounded in a gas attack in late 1918.

Uecker River: River in northeastern Germany that runs by Pasewalk.

Ors: A small village in northeastern France where Wilfred Owen is buried.

Koksijde: Flemish town in Belgium and the burial place of the remains of T. E. Hulme.

Tartarus: In Greek myth, it is the part of the underworld where souls go to be judged.

To the Island of Philoctetes

The book referenced in the subtitle is Christopher Hassell's *Rupert Brooke* (New York: Harcourt, Brace and World, 1964).

Philoctetes was the Greek hero who had inherited the bow of Heracles (see above). Rupert Brooke, who had volunteered to go with the British Expeditionary Force to the Mediterranean during the early stages of World War I, was bitten by a mosquito at camp in Egypt. An infection from this bite, along with sunstroke and dysentery, led him to be hospitalized at Port Saïd. But when his unit departed for

Lemnos to prepare for the campaign, Brooke decided to go, too. It was likely a fatal mistake. After his ship arrived at Lemnos, it was redirected to the smaller island of Skyros. Brooke died from an infection on a French hospital ship off the coast and is buried on Skyros.

Brooke's boyhood nickname was "Oyster."

On a visit to Lancaster, Pa., I saw a "deep-tanned" and barefoot Amish girl working in her garden. She was wearing a straw hat much like the one in which Brooke's Tahitian lover, Taatamata, is pictured.

"The songstress's voice": In June 1913, as part of his visit to the United States, Brooke took a canoe trip down the Delaware with the New York lawyer Russell Loines. As he reported to Cathleen Nesbitt, "we came round a wild turn in the river, and there was a voice singing wonderfully . . . we saw a little house, high on the bank, with an orchard, and a verandah, and wooden steps down to the great river, and at the top of them was a tall girl, very beautiful, standing like a goddess, with wonderful red hair, her head thrown back, singing, singing . . ."

In 1913, Brooke visited Tahiti.

Frances Cornford, née Darwin: A close friend of Brooke, Cornford was a poet and the granddaughter of Charles Darwin. The reference is to her poem "Wartime Sketch."

> Drink the unflowing waters with green hair
> You Cambridge willows, calm and unaware;
> Soon he will vanish like a summer's midge,
> That calm-struck soldier leaning on the bridge,
> And things be always as they always were.

Reflections on Reflections

The book referenced in the subtitle is Jan Marsh's *Edward Thomas: A Poet for His Country* (New York: Barnes & Noble, 1978).

The Helen referred to is Helen Noble, with whom Thomas had an affair and who became pregnant, resulting shortly after in their marriage. There are, of course, the obvious classical connotations to the name.

Sandspring Drive, Eatontown, the home of the author at present.

The poets Robert Frost, Lascelles Abercrombie, Rupert Brooke, and Wilfred Gibson.

"Bu" was the nickname of the great jazz drummer Art Blakey—a short form of his Muslim name, Buhaina.

55 refers to the famous 55 Bar, a jazz club on Christopher Street in New York City.

Sand in My Pocket

The book referenced in the subtitle is Alun Jones's *The Life and Opinions of T. E. Hulme* (Boston: Beacon Press, 1960).

The Bridge of Sighs is a stone-covered bridge at St. John's College, Cambridge, designed by Henry Hutchinson and erected in 1831 over the River Cam. It's named after the more famous bridge in Venice.

The Belvedere is a part of the Vatican where Leonardo da Vinci stayed as a guest while Raphael and Michelangelo were doing their great works for Pope Julius II. Although the pope and his successor showed Leonardo respect, they did not offer him any commissions.

Singing from a Lower Branch

The book referenced in the subtitle is Dominic Hibberd's *Wilfred Owen: A New Biography* (Chicago: Ivan R. Dee, 2002).

When Owen was living in Dunsden, a horrific accident took place in which horses pulling a cart with a family and furnishings aboard bolted. The mother and one daughter were killed and a second young daughter was severely injured when they were thrown from the cart.

The "broad red veranda" is the rocking-chair-filled porch at Ron's West End Pub, Long Branch, N.J.

Struck from the Chill of the World

The reading referenced in the subtitle is Jean Moorcroft Wilson's *Isaac Rosenberg: The Making of a Great War Poet: A New Life* (Evanston, Ill.: Northwestern University Press, 2008).

"Crane's urchins": The reference is to Hart Crane's "Voyages."

William Waterworth (1889–1963): My great-grandfather from Preston, England, who served in Salonika with the 346th Motor Transport Co. of the Royal Army Service Corps.

Bibliography

Sandra Casey to Karen L. Weeks, 13 January 2020.

Brooke, Rupert, *Collected Poems of Rupert Brooke* (New York: Dodd, Mead, and Co., 1915).
Dedijer, Vladimir, *The Road to Sarajevo* (New York: Simon & Schuster, 1966).
Fergusson, Robert, *The Short Sharp Life of T. E. Hulme* (London: Allen Lane, 2002).
Gilbert, Martin, *The Somme: Heroism and Horror in the First World War* (New York: Henry Holt & Co., 2006).
Hassell, Christopher, *Rupert Brooke* (New York: Harcourt, Brace and World, 1964).
Hibberd, Dominic, *Wilfred Owen: A New Biography* (Chicago: Ivan R. Dee, 2003).
Jones, Alun, *The Life and Opinions of T. E. Hulme* (Boston: Beacon Press, 1960).
Keegan, John, *An Illustrated History of the First World War* (New York: Alfred A. Knopf, 2001).
Marsh, Jan, *Edward Thomas: A Poet for His Country* (New York: Barnes & Noble, 1978).
Owen, Wilfred, *Collected Poems* (New York: New Directions, 1963).
Owen, Wilfred, *Collected Letters*, ed. Harold Owen and John Bell (London: Oxford University Press, 1967).
Parker, Newton C., "Paris Knows Few Equals to Her Wilson Welcome," *Nashville Banner*, 15 Dec. 1918.
Parsons, Ian, ed., *The Collected Works of Isaac Rosenberg: Poetry, Prose Letters, Paintings and Drawings* (New York: Oxford University Press, 1979).
Powell, E. Alexander, *Fighting in Flanders* (New York: Charles Scribner's Sons, 1914).
Thomas, Edward, *The Diary of Edward Thomas, 1 January-8 April 1917* (Andoversford, U.K: Whittington Press, 1977).
———*The Works of Edward Thomas* (Ware, U.K.: Wordsworth Library, 1994).
Van der Kiste, John, *Kaiser Wilhelm II: Germany's Last Emperor* (Phoenix Mill, U.K.: Sutton Publishing, 1999).
Wilson, Jean Moorcroft, *Isaac Rosenberg: The Making of a Great War Poet: A New Life* (Evanston, Ill.: Northwestern University Press, 2008).

About the Author

Daniel Weeks has published eight previous collections of poetry, including *For Now: New and Collected Poems, 1979-2017*. His poems have appeared in literary journals across the United States. Weeks is currently editor of *This Broken Shore*, a literary magazine featuring New Jersey-connected writers. He is also the author of *Gateways to Empire: Quebec and New Amsterdam to 1664*, *Nearer Home: Short Histories, 1987-2019*, *A More Prosaic Light: Essays, Revisions, and Reviews, 1987-2015*, and *Not for Filthy Lucre's Sake: Richard Saltar and the Antiproprietary Movement in East New Jersey, 1665-1707*.

www.ingramcontent.com/pod-product-compliance
Lightning Source LLC
Chambersburg PA
CBHW031320160426
43196CB00007B/604